ACTING

LIKE

CHRISTIANS

By

Ruth Huston

BRYAN COLLEGE

Dayton, Tennessee 37321

Dedicated to and presented to

Bryan College

to be used for the glory of God

ACTING LIKE CHRISTIANS
Copyright 1972 by
Bryan College
Dayton, Tennessee 37321

Body type in this book is 10-point Century
Composition, layout, and design
by
Word Systems, Inc.
Dayton, Tennessee 37321

Printed in the United States of America
by
College Press
Collegedale, Tennessee 37315

FOREWORD

There should be a purpose for writing a book and a reading audience for whom the book is written.

My purpose in writing this book has been to find out for myself from the New Testament how a Christian should act and to share with any or all interested persons what I found. Because I have been puzzled, disturbed, and often misled by the behavior of some people who called themselves "Christians," I decided to look through my New Testament to see how I, a Christian, should act during the rest of my days here on earth. This book is hopefully the answer to those who, like myself, want to be genuine Christians by God's standards. The measurement or yardstick of perfection is found in the Person of His Son, the Man named Jesus.

There have been problems in choosing a title that would catch people's attention and interest them in reading the book. After many ideas and suggestions, when I hovered between the words "behave" or "act" and "like" or "as," one night on the radio program "The Hour of Decision," I heard Dr. Billy Graham say about someone he had talked with: "You say you are a Christian. Then why don't you act like one?" I knew then that I had my title, the correct title to reveal the contents of this book.

The book contains Bible study, illustrations, and verses from favorite hymns or poems, which are my way of expressing my knowledge and love of God in Christ Jesus.

Much of my reading audience will, I hope, be my mountain friends among whom I have lived for many years and to whom I have taught the Bible. Many of these readers will, I hope, be campers who have attended camp at Camp Nathanael at Emmalena, Kentucky, and who will want the answer to some of the questions they have about Christian living.

I have tried to write in simple, plain language in order that no reader will miss the point of what I have been trying to say. I have used the King James Version of the Bible in my quotations. However, as I have tried to understand the meaning of words or phrases, I have done a great deal of research by reading in commentaries, concordances, dictionaries, and modern versions of the New Testament.

I want to say "Thank you" to the many people who have helped and encouraged me to complete the book and make it available to the public. There have been those who have helped by typing, especially Mrs. Carl G. Eshleman of Coatesville, Pennsylvania, who did a beautiful job with the manuscript. I am grateful to the friends at Bryan College in Dayton, Tennessee, who offered to take the responsibility of publishing the book, and to Mrs. Theodore C. Mercer, the president's wife, who spent many, many hours editing and improving the manuscript.

For all the readers of this book, it is my hope and desire that, as you read the pages and the chapters, the Holy Spirit will be able to show you how to be free from all preconceived ideas, prejudice, unbelief, and blindness toward God's Word. Then with His help you can see (as I have) God's truth revealed in Christ Jesus and know that through receiving Jesus into your heart as your Savior, trusting and obeying Him as your Lord, you can be a genuine Christian. People will sense the presence of the Lord Jesus Christ in your life and will know that you belong to Him, are walking "as he walked" and are walking "in him."

Ruth Huston

May, 1972
Emmalena, Kentucky

TABLE OF CONTENTS

ACTING LIKE CHRISTIANS

CHAPTER ONE

Toward

The Bible–God's Word

God hath spoken." These words ring out from the pages of the Holy Scriptures. God speaks to people today through the Bible. It is His word to mankind, given by inspiration to writers chosen by Him to communicate His truth. "All scripture is given by inspiration of God" (II Timothy 3:16). It lasts forever: "The Word of the Lord endureth forever" (I Peter 1:25). Christians believe the Bible to be inspired because God says so and because it inspires them. In Hebrews 1:1 the Holy Spirit, through the writer, says: "God . . . spake in time past unto the fathers by the prophets." These words tell all who are interested that the Old Testament is God's Word. In Hebrews 1:2 again the Holy Spirit (and this time referring to the New Testament) says: "[God] hath in these last days spoken unto us by his Son."

Jesus, in no uncertain tones, told the believers after His resurrection, in Luke 24:27, that the Old Testament writers spoke of Him: "And beginning at Moses and all the prophets, He expounded unto them, in all the scriptures, the things concerning Himself." Later in verse 44 He said, "These are the words which I spake unto you while I was yet with you that all things must be fulfilled which were written in the law of Moses and in the prophets and in the psalms concerning me." In other words Jesus made it plain that the Old Testament writers foretold His coming: what He would be like, what He would do, and what would happen to Him.

Peter said about the Old Testament writers, in II Peter 1:21: "For the prophecy came not in old time by the will of man but holy men of God spake as they were moved by the Holy Ghost

1

[Spirit]." John, the disciple who loved Jesus so much, said, in I John 5:11, "This is the record [the New Testament message], that God hath given to us eternal life, and this life is in his Son." Jesus Himself made it very clear that the words He said were given to Him by His Father in heaven: "The words that I speak unto you, I speak not of myself; but the Father that dwelleth in me" (John 14:10). On the Mount of Transfiguration God spoke out of a cloud to Peter, James, and John: "This is my beloved Son; hear him" (Luke 9:35).

The words of Jesus are "spirit" and "life" (John 6:63). An Indian Christian, Sundar Singh, said, "I have found my Saviour to be exactly the same as recorded in this book. He has been to me all that we read concerning Him there. Language difficulties . . . have not hidden its truth nor hindered in the least its lifegiving influence in my heart; because of these words 'they are spirit and they are life.' In reading the Bible I have found such untold and eternal wealth of riches. In passing on its message to others, and sharing it with them, its blessing to me, and to them, continually increases."

> Tell me the old, old story,
> Of unseen things above,
> Of Jesus and His glory,
> Of Jesus and His love.

A great educator, William Lyons Phelps of Yale, said, "If it were a choice between a knowledge of the Bible and a college education, I would choose the Bible."

In this Bible we find the gospel message, or good news, by which we have been saved. Paul writes in I Corinthians 15:1-4, of "the gospel which I preached unto you, which also ye have received, and wherein ye stand; by which also ye are saved." Paul claimed that he received his knowledge by revelation and not, as some say, because he had a guilt complex from killing so many Christians. And what is the gospel? "Christ died for our sins according to the scriptures; And that he was buried and that he rose again the third day, according to the scriptures" (verses 3, 4). The preaching of that message by Paul, in demonstration of the Spirit and of power, to the Corinthians resulted in their faith, standing not "in the wisdom of men, but in the power of God" (I Corinthians 2:4, 5).

2

This passage thrilled me when I first discovered it for myself. I delighted to know that I was able to stand not in the wisdom of men, which confused me, but in the power of God.

The gospel "is the power of God unto salvation to everyone that believeth" (Romans 1:16). Every true Christian knows this. Every true Christian can and should have the assurance of this wonderful salvation.

> How firm a foundation,
> Ye saints of the Lord,
> Is laid for your faith
> In His excellent Word!

As a young Christian I frequently went forward in evangelistic meetings to become sure of my salvation and was never satisfied. A speaker at a Bible conference one summer spoke on John 5:24. As he explained the meaning of that verse, I received the needed assurance because I realized I had done what Jesus said: I had heard His Word; believed on God, who sent Him; had received everlasting life; and had indeed "passed from death unto life." Another verse that settled the matter was John 1:12. I had received Jesus Christ and had become a child of God, because I had believed on His name.

> I know not how this saving faith
> To me He did impart,
> Nor how believing in His Word
> Wrought peace within my heart.

> I know not how the Spirit moves,
> Convincing men of sin,
> Revealing Jesus through the Word,
> Creating faith in Him.

> But "I know Whom I have believed,
> And am persuaded
> That He is able
> To keep that which I've committed
> Unto Him against that day."

What are some of the other things the Bible does for us? The Thessalonian Christians received the preaching of Paul as the Word of God, which Paul said, "worketh effectually also in you that believe." It is a life changer.

A little Christian woman was facing a surgical operation. To comfort herself, she was looking up some of the "fear not's" of the Bible. Her surgeon noticed what she was doing as he passed her bed in the ward and laughed at her for believing the Bible, which he said was no longer read or believed by most people. During the course of the conversation, he told her that he once had believed but had lost his faith and sometimes wished he had the simple faith of his youth once more. With a cheering remark he turned on his heel and left her bedside. The patient forgot her need for encouragement for herself and kept thinking of him and the wistful look on his face as he spoke of his lost faith. She found herself praying for him, asking her heavenly Father to restore to him childlike faith in Jesus Christ. As she went under the anesthetic she repeated the words of Jesus: "I have prayed for thee that thy faith fail not." After the operation the nurse told her that, under the influence of the anesthetic, she sang the hymn "Abide With Me" right through, and all in the operating room were deeply moved, including the surgeon. What a joy it was days later when the doctor came to her and whispered, "It's all right, little woman. I have gotten back to my old sweet faith in God and the Bible. What you said and sang under the anesthetic set me thinking, and I could not rest until I found my faith of other days."

> Sing them over again to me,
> Wonderful words of Life;
> Let me more of their beauty see,
> Wonderful words of Life.
> Words of life and beauty,
> Teach me faith and duty;
> Beautiful words, wonderful words,
> Wonderful words of Life.

Another thing the Bible does for us is to produce Christian character in our lives. Jesus revealed by His life what Christians should be like. He said: "I am the vine, ye are the branches: He that abideth in me and I in him the same bringeth forth much

4

fruit: for without me, ye can do nothing" (John 15:5). That fruit is likeness to Jesus Christ: "The fruit of the spirit is love, joy, peace, longsuffering, gentleness, goodness, faith, meekness, temperance" (Galatians 5:22, 23). It is Jesus' character formed in the believer. In explaining the parable of the seed and the sower, Jesus said: "He that received seed into the good ground is he that heareth the word and understandeth it, which also beareth fruit . . . " (Matthew 13:23).

Here are apt words from the hymn "More About Jesus Would I Know":

> More about Jesus in His word,
> Holding communion with my Lord;
> Hearing His voice in ev'ry line,
> Making each faithful saying mine.

What are some of the responsibilities we have toward God's Word? First of all we must read or listen to it, for "faith cometh by hearing and hearing by the word of God" (Romans 10:17). We must read it reverently, prayerfully, regularly, and respectfully. In Acts 17:11 and 12, the Bereans received the word with all readiness of mind, searched it daily, and many of them believed. To the Thessalonians the gospel came not only in word, but in power, in the Holy Ghost (Spirit) and in much assurance (or certainty), and was received with joy (I Thessalonians 1:5, 6). The Bible is a holy book and should be approached reverently, not carelessly.

Paul prayed that the Ephesian Christians might have the eyes of their understanding enlightened by the spirit of wisdom and revelation in the knowledge of God (Ephesians 1:17, 18). Asking the Holy Spirit to help us understand what is being read is a very important part of our daily Bible reading.

> Open my eyes, that I may see
> Glimpses of truth Thou hast for me . . . .
> Open my eyes, illumine me,
> Spirit Divine.

The Bible is today being translated into many different languages in order that people of different tongues may be able to

5

have a knowledge of God's truths by reading it with understanding, in their own words.

Not long ago the first Bible in the Lisu language reached Burma. The recipient, Pastor Lucius, wrote: "Hallelujah! Praise and thanks be to God our Father. In order that He may have fellowship with us men of earth and might be able to instruct us He has given us His very precious and great Holy Book, that which we have mourned for with tears and longing, hoping and praying, God has granted. On the evening of October 4th my own eyes saw and my own hands held His Holy Word. My heart is filled with joy; my whole being is filled with satisfaction.

"Everyone who heard the news came running into my home. When they saw, they jumped up and clapped their hands. So filled with abounding joy were we all that we literally jumped and hopped around because we had received what we had longed to see and longed to touch. This is the most precious thing upon this globe. Even if someone would offer me in exchange a thousand kingdoms like this whole, wide world, I would never accept and never exchange. Long before daylight I was up, reading, and this morning too, I was up at first cockcrow reading and reading."

> We've a story to tell to the nations
> That shall turn their hearts to the right,
> A story of truth and mercy,
> A story of peace and light.
>
> We've a Savior to show to the nations
> Who the path of sorrow hath trod,
> That all of the world's great peoples
> Might come to the truth of God.

In Revelation 1:3, John writes: "Blessed is he that readeth, and they that hear the words of this prophecy, and keep those things which are written therein . . . ." Blessing comes not only to those who read, but to those who hear the Word of God. Today tremendous strides are being made through radio, recording, television, and translation in the effort to reach the still unreached by allowing them to hear God's message in their own language.

Another thing God's Word will do is to build us up in the faith: "And now, brethren, I commend you to God and to the word of his grace, which is able to build you up" (Acts 20:32). If we are to know the Bible we must study it: "Study to shew thyself approved unto God, a workman that needeth not to be ashamed, rightly dividing the word of truth" (II Timothy 2:15). It must be studied to be used with skill and to the very best advantage.

A well-known Bible teacher has said: "When one has a knowledge of God's Word he can be useful and helpful to those around. A knowledge of the Bible equips Spirit-filled believers to point lost and dying men to Christ."

My father, a Christian businessman, diligently studied the Bible to know and understand it and to use it in his witness for his Lord. He wanted to know how to tell the Gospel, the Good News, to those who were lost.

When my Scottish grandfather was dying in Savannah, Georgia, it was my father who was able to explain the way of salvation to him. My mother, who dearly loved her father, had for a long time fasted and prayed every Friday for his salvation, but was unable to lead him to Christ. The "do not's" of the religion he had been taught in his home in Scotland had turned him against Christianity.

It was on a Friday when my father, with Bible in hand, sat at my grandfather's bedside and explained from John 3:14-16 what Jesus, because of God's great love, had done for him. As Father told the story of Moses, in the wilderness, lifting up the brazen serpent on a pole so that sinning Israelites might look at it by faith and live, and related that story to the lifting up of Christ on the cross for sinners (including my grandfather), light came to Grandfather's face as he said, "I see it! I see it!" From that moment to the day of his death, he proved by his words, public confession of faith, baptism, and partaking of the Lord's Supper that the message of the Scriptures had brought salvation to him.

> Tell me the story slowly,
> That I may take it in—
> That wonderful redemption,
> God's remedy for sin.

A knowledge of the Bible makes us aware of sin. The owner of a motel told a guest who asked why she had a Gideon Bible on a table in every room, "Do you want to know something? I find when I keep the Bible out where people can see it, fewer of my towels are stolen!"

One of the most important responsibilities we have toward the Bible is to obey what it says. In John 14:31, Jesus said, "As the Father gave me commandment, even so I do." Jesus' example is what we are to follow. A lady went to her Christian friend with a complaint that she found no pleasure in reading the Bible and that it seemed to do her no good any more. "Go home," he advised her, "and open your New Testament, read until you come to a commandment, then close the book and obey what you have read. After you have obeyed, read on until you come to the next commandment and do likewise with that." A few weeks later she came back, with her face aglow, and said, "I want to thank you for the help you gave me. The Bible is a new book to me now."

In Matthew 7:24, 25, Jesus makes it plain that the wise man who builds his house on a rock is the one who hears Jesus' sayings and "doeth" them. Those who are truly related to Him, in Luke 8:21, are those who hear the Word of God and do it. In John 13:17, Jesus said to His listeners: "If ye know these things, happy are ye if ye do them." In other words, we must practice obeying what Christ has said so plainly. Some other verses on this subject are James 1:22, "Be ye doers of the word, and not hearers only, deceiving your own selves"; II Peter 1:19, "We have also a more sure word of prophecy; whereunto ye do well that ye take heed, as unto a light that shineth in a dark place, until the day dawn, and the day star arise in your hearts"; and, finally, I John 2:5, "Whoso keepeth his word, in him verily is the love of God perfected; hereby know we that we are in him." The test of our love for God is our obedience to His revealed commands.

> When we walk with the Lord
> In the light of His Word,
> What a glory He sheds on our way!
> While we do His good will,
> He abides with us still,
> And with all who will trust and obey.
>
> Trust and obey,
> For there's no other way,
> To be happy in Jesus,
> But to trust and obey.

We should meditate upon God's Word (I Timothy 4:15). Not only should we read or listen to it prayerfully, respectfully, and regularly, but we should know it, study it, and obey it. We should concentrate at length on portions of Scripture. If we have only ten or fifteen minutes a day, we should read our Bibles thoughtfully and consecutively to get a grasp of the whole counsel of God. As a cow chews her cud, we should go over and over some portion, wait, ponder and pray, compare Scripture with Scripture; and the Word will become ours. When we see a verse that fits our need or shows us the wonder of God's love and purpose for us, we will be fully repaid for the time spent.

"Is this God's book?" asked a little boy. "Yes, son," replied his mother. "Don't you think we should send it back," he asked, "if we don't read it?"

The Bible is the Lord's book for us and we need it. Without food from the Bible we will be weak and unhappy. We must feed on the promises of God, such as "I will never leave thee nor forsake thee"; "Lo, I am with you alway"; "Come unto me and I will give you rest"; "He that cometh unto me shall never hunger and he that believeth on me shall never thirst"; "I go to prepare a place for you; I will come again and receive you unto myself that where I am there ye may be also"; and many more that bring comfort, refreshing, encouragement, and hope for today and tomorrow.

> Standing on the promises that cannot fail,
> When the howling storms of doubt and fear assail,
> By the living Word of God I shall prevail,
> Standing on the promises of God.

A woman became greatly troubled over a loved one, a Christian, in whom she had found unexpected weaknesses. One day while she was reading her Bible, a verse (Acts 3:16) leaped out of the pages at her: "And his name through faith in his name hath made this man strong, whom ye see and know: yea, the faith which is by him hath given him this perfect soundness in the presence of you all."

She knew this was God's promise to her and it brought peace of mind, courage, and faith to wait for Him to do what no one else could possibly accomplish. The years went by—years of trial, testing, heartache, and waiting patiently for the answer, which did not come. The Lord had set no time for the miracle. She had to continue to trust Him and believe His word to her. When the answer finally came, she was filled with relief and gladness of heart to see that loved one come out of weakness into the strength of the Lord. She had experienced anew that God keeps His promises to those who count on Him. When He gives a promise He will fulfill it. We must believe Him until the answer comes.

We should memorize Scriptures that will come back in times of need: "Let the word of Christ dwell in you richly in all wisdom" (Colossians 3:16). For effective Christian service and daily living, we need God's Word, "the sword of the Spirit" in our minds for protection against Satan and for the message others need for salvation and every sort of help.

When the devil tempted Jesus on the Mount of Temptation, He answered him from the Scriptures, "It is written" (Matthew 4: 4, 7, 10) and won the victory over the tempter. The Word of God must be used. We must know it to be able to use it, "holding forth the word of life" (Philippians 2:16). It is the message of eternal life. We must use it prayerfully, depending on the Holy Spirit to bring the right verses to mind, that it "may have free course [be unhindered] and be glorified" (II Thessalonians 3:1).

One of the best illustrations on the use of a Bible verse to overcome Satan is in my first book, *God's Timing*. This story happened in the early days of our ministry at Camp Nathanael, located at Emmalena in the Kentucky Mountains.

One night when a week of camp was half over, some of the workers decided it would be fun to go frog hunting in Troublesome Creek after the campers quieted down in their tents.

A summer worker, an athletic college girl, felt she was strong enough to stand anything, even though all her strength was needed to help with strenuous recreation the following day. So she went along with the crowd.

Because her brother skinned snakes for a hobby, she had a terrific fear of them. When one of the fellows shot a snake in the water, she determined to overcome her fear by grabbing the tail and dragging the snake through the water to the bank of the creek. Reflex action caused the snake to move. This frightened her. To calm her fear, another worker stepped on the snake's head and crushed it on a rock with her heel.

Then Milly took the dead snake out of the water and laid it on the creek bank. The odor of the snake on her hand horrified her; so she tried to wash it off. Because this was not very successful she went to her tent and threw herself on her cot in wet clothes.

Like someone in a trance she kept weeping and crying out hysterically about snakes. No one could calm her, and the noise was disturbing those near her. When anyone would pray or mention the name of Jesus, she would become worse; and those in the tent with her felt the power of Satan.

As they could accomplish nothing by persuasion or prayer, one of them came to the tent where two of us were sound asleep and woke us up to tell us about their problem and ask our advice.

We had a word of prayer, asking God to overrule this attack. Then it occurred to us that we were right in the middle of a week of camp, when the Holy Spirit usually started working, and this was the devil attacking and hindering. A verse of Scripture came to me and we suggested that the young girl be urged to repeat the words of the verse and take her stand upon II Timothy 1:7: "For God hath not given us the spirit of fear; but of power, and of love, and of a sound mind."

After many unsuccessful attempts, for she would break down, cry, and refuse to finish the verse (we could hear the workers repeating, "Say it, Milly, say it!"), she finally got through the whole verse and went off into a peaceful sleep for the rest of the night. The power of Satan was broken by the use of the Word.

The next morning we were exhausted, but she was not and commented on the fact and that she felt fine. She seemed to remember nothing about the snake episode and no one mentioned it. At the usual testimony meeting at the end of the week, Milly got up and amazed us by quoting II Timothy 1:7 as a verse that had become very real to her. It turned out that she could remember nothing between the time of placing the snake on the bank and the next morning when she woke up for another day's work at camp. Needless to say, the Lord worked in the hearts of the campers, and many made decisions for Christ that week.

> Thy Word is a lamp to my feet,
> A light to my path alway,
> To guide and to save me from sin,
> And show me the heav'nly way.[1]

11

Forever, O Lord, is Thy Word
Established and fixed on high;
Thy faithfulness unto all men
Abideth forever nigh.

Thy Word have I hid in my heart,
That I might not sin against Thee,
That I might not sin,
That I might not sin,
Thy Word have I hid in my heart.

In the Bible we find:

The way into God's family	John 1:12
The assurance of having everlasting life	John 5:24
The way to grow strong:	
(1) desire the milk of the Word	I Peter 2:2
(2) desire the strong meat of it	Hebrews 5:12-14
The knowledge of the truth that brings freedom	John 8:31, 32
The perfect law of liberty (love)	James 1:25
Exceeding great and precious promises	II Peter 1:4
How to pray	Mark 11:22, 24
How to be happy	John 13:17
How to be successful in forming Christian character	Luke 8:15
How to live with other Christians	Colossians 3:16
How to invest our lives	Acts 20:32
How to succeed	Philippians 2:16
How to win over Satan	Ephesians 6:11
How to know the future	II Peter 1:19

What are some of the results of acting like Christians toward the Bible when it is read, listened to, believed, revered, respected, loved, and obeyed?

There are the following results:

Assurance of salvation	John 5:24
Faith to act upon what God has said	Romans 10:17
An enlightened mind—the mind of Christ	I Corinthians 2:16
	Philippians 2:5
The knowledge of God's will	Romans 12:2
The blessing of doing God's will	James 1:22, 25
An effectual working in our lives	I Thessalonians 2:13
A fruitful life	John 15:5
Love	John 17:26
Joy	John 15:11
Peace	John 14:27
Hope of heaven	Colossians 1:5
Fellowship with God	I John 1:3
Fellowship with like-minded believers	I John 1:7
Purity of life	John 17:17
Happiness	John 13:17
Sin revealed in our lives	Romans 7:22, 23
Victory over sin	Romans 7:24, 25
God's way of deliverance	I John 1:9
Freedom from self	John 8:36
Knowing how to secure answers to prayer	John 15:7
Knowing how to grow strong in the faith	Acts 20:32
Freedom from false teaching	I John 4:1, 2
	John 8:32
Knowledge of God's love and multiplied blessings	John 17:3, 8, 26
Knowledge of the glorious future that awaits us with rewards for faithfulness	Titus 2:13
	Revelation 22:12

Oh, the power of the Word of God!
What comfort it provides!
And what joy it gives to our hearts!

Go to the Word of God and see for yourself what the Bible will
do for your life if you permit the Christ of the Bible to live in and
through you.

Thy Word is like a garden, Lord,
With flowers bright and fair;
And everyone who seeks may pluck
A lovely cluster there.
Thy Word is like a deep, deep mine;
And jewels rich and rare
Are hidden in its mighty depths
For every searcher there.

Thy Word is like a starry host:
A thousand rays of light
Are seen to guard the traveler,
And make his pathway bright,
Thy Word is like an armory,
Where soldiers may repair,
And find, for life's long battle day,
All needful weapons there.

O may I love Thy precious Word,
May I explore the mine,
May I its fragrant flowers glean,
May light upon me shine.
O may I find my armor there,
Thy Word my trusty sword;
I'll learn to fight with every foe
The battle of the Lord.

CHAPTER TWO

Toward

The Trinity—God in Three Persons

W e learned from Chapter One that the Bible is God's Word to
man. God has spoken and in His Word He has told us many
things about Himself and about people.

In the first verse of the Bible, God, the Creator (Genesis 1:1),
revealed Himself as a God who is not a single person. In
Genesis 1:26 God said, "Let us make man in our image, after our
likeness." He used the pronouns "us" and "our."

In all the Scriptures God shows Himself to be three Persons in
one. This is a mystery (I Timothy 3:16), but a fact. My dictionary
tells me that the word "mystery" in theology is "any assumed
truth that cannot be comprehended by the human mind but must
be accepted on faith," and that a "fact" is a "thing that is true"!

I became curious about the meaning of the words "person" and
"people." This is what I found. "Persons" are personalities—
individuals "distinctly different from one another." "People" are
human beings with individual personalities and are "distinct from
other animals."

God is a "Person," but He is not "people." "People" are
"persons," but they are not God.

God is three Persons in one. Each Person in the Godhead is
distinctly different from "people" in that the Father, the Son, and
the Holy Spirit have "divine qualities," and people have not.
Adam, the first man, sinned and lost those divine qualities—God's
"image" and God's "likeness."

The marvelous thing is that God came down to earth in the
Person of His Son and indwelt a human body, the body of Jesus of
Nazareth. For almost twenty centuries He has been dwelling in

human bodies, the bodies of those "people" who have received His Son, Jesus Christ, into their hearts. (More about this in Chapter Three.)

It is a fact, "a thing that is true," that God made man in His likeness, an intelligent, spiritual creature with whom He desired to have fellowship and companionship. Man was made like God in that He made him spirit, soul, and body—a tri-partite being (I Thessalonians 5:23).

God desires worship, praise, and adoration for Himself for what He is and what He has done for us.

This triune God is recognized in Christian gatherings by the singing of the familiar Doxology:

> Praise God, from whom all blessings flow;
> Praise Him, all creatures here below;
> Praise Him above, ye heavenly host;
> Praise Father, Son, and Holy Ghost!

These words have tremendous meaning, but seldom do people think of what they are singing. The mind wanders to every other interest or person; and the heart is empty of all feeling toward a wonderful, loving, kind God.

This triune God has blessings untold to give to His own. These blessings flow, moving gently and steadily like a stream toward its destination to be poured out upon and to give refreshing to "all creatures here below." "Blessed be the God and Father of our Lord Jesus Christ, who hath blessed us with all spiritual blessings in heavenly places in Christ" (Ephesians 1:3). "Every good gift and every perfect gift is from above, and cometh down from the Father of lights, with whom is no variableness, neither shadow of turning" (James 1:17).

According to the dictionary a "blessing" is "anything that gives happiness or prevents misfortune, to make prosperous, to guard and preserve, to bring comfort, approval, bliss and good fortune." Blessing comes from someone who takes an interest in a person, feels for that person, wishes well to that person, wants to aid, benefit or give comfort to that person. That someone has grace, charity, and mercy toward another. Such is God, the Creator; "Therefore let us offer the sacrifice of praise to God continually, that is, the fruit of our lips giving thanks to His name."

16

O worship the King, all-glorious above,
O gratefully sing His power and His love;
Our Shield and Defender, the Ancient of Days,
Pavilioned in splendor, and girded with praise.

A story has been told of a highlight in American history. In the year 1952 an exhausted General Dwight D. Eisenhower and his beloved Mamie were returning from a strenuous presidential campaign in New England. They were in the dirty, dimly lighted club car of a railroad train that had pulled out of the Boston station at midnight. With them were some dog-tired, sleep-starved newspaper writers and orchestra leader Fred Waring, who was accompanied by a few talented singers from his excellent choir. Fred Waring was exhausted. He needed a shave. His clothes were rumpled, as were those of his entertainers. Mamie in her own words was "bushed." The general was silent. He looked as if he had been through an ordeal. The appearances of the reporters were beyond description.

Someone suggested a song, and Waring conducted the motley "choir" through favorites, such as "Mamie" and "The Sunshine of Your Smile."

The hour was late. The general looked at his watch and asked for one more song before retiring. Waring stood up, held up his arms, gave the familiar downbeat, and a couple of professionals seated on the floor in the other end of the crowded car started out:

"Our Father which art in heaven . . . ." A few of the car lights blinked, screeching noises were heard, but on it went. By the time the song got to "Thy kingdom come," the Eisenhowers had started to sing. At "Give us this day," all had joined in.

A noisy train rushing past to Boston, an ash tray toppling over as they rounded a curve did not stop the singers: " . . . but deliver us from evil."

Rain and sleet beating against the windows almost drowned out words, but the song continued.

With smiles of approval and expert direction, Fred Waring drew out a climactic "Amen."

There was silence for a few seconds. Then the Eisenhowers stood up, smiled in gratitude at Waring and his "choir," and went off to their car.

Everyone else went off to bed too, with the sound of great words, well sung, still ringing: "For Thine is the kingdom, and the power and the glory forever."

The Trinity is mentioned in several passages in the New Testament. In Matthew 3:16, 17, there is the voice of the Father from heaven; the Son, Jesus, standing by the Jordan River; and the Spirit of God descending from heaven like a dove. In Matthew 28: 19 we read that the disciples were told to baptize "in the name of the Father and of the Son and of the Holy Ghost [Spirit]." Paul gives a familiar benediction in II Corinthians 13:14: "the grace of the Lord Jesus Christ, and the love of God, and the communion of the Holy Ghost [Spirit] be with you all."

We are told that God is a Spirit to be worshiped (John 4:24). God is a Person to be known (John 17:3). Though unseen, He is real. He is a personality who has life in Himself (John 5:26). He is not dead, He lives!

How does God reveal His personality? In the creation account He "said," He "saw," He "divided," He "called" (or named), He "made," He "set them [sun, moon and stars] in the firmament of the heaven," He "created," He "blessed," He "rested."

God can hear. In Genesis 4:10 He heard from heaven. He will hear from heaven: "If we ask anything according to His will he heareth us" (I John 5:14). He can smell: "And the Lord smelled a sweet savour . . . " (Genesis 8:21). God knows: He "knoweth all things" (I John 3:20). God thinks: "For I know the thoughts that I think toward you," saith the Lord, "thoughts of peace and not of evil" (Jeremiah 29:11).

What kind of Person is the God of the Bible? He is holy. In the Lord's prayer Jesus taught the disciples to pray: "Our Father, which art in heaven, hallowed be thy name." God is above all. God is sinless. God is all good. Because God is holy every Christian ought to worship Him. "Worship" is "showing reverence, love, and admiration to another person—mainly to God."

> Holy, Holy, Holy, Lord God Almighty!
> Early in the morning our song shall rise to Thee;
> Holy, Holy, Holy! Merciful and Mighty!
> God in Three Persons, blessed Trinity!

How are we as Christians to act toward this holy God, who desires our worship and who only is worthy to receive it? We must recognize God's holiness and go to Him reverently, in awe, with respect and not carelessly or lightly. We must honor His holy name. We must praise Him from the heart. We must want to communicate with God as another personality who waits for true fellowship. God longs to be more than an acquaintance. God wants His own really to know Him as He is (I John 1:1-3). There is no greater joy than this. David said, "In thy presence is fullness of joy."

To know a person intimately, one must cultivate that friendship. It takes effort and perseverance. Jesus prayed for His own: "That they might know thee, the only true God." This prayer of His will be answered in the life of every believer who comes really to know God. In order to know Him as Father, we must obey Him. "We do know that we know Him if we keep His commandments" (I John 2:3). We can become better acquainted with Him only by practicing His rules. Those rules are not too difficult for any believer.

Persons can learn to know each other by constant daily companionship and sharing of thoughts and interests; otherwise they have a distorted or unrealistic picture of each other. Many Christians have a false picture of God. They make Him to suit their own particular thought and need. Through prayer to Him, through careful, open-minded study of the Bible, honestly looking for His Personality all through the Scriptures to see what He is like, how He acts, what He thinks, what He wants, what He plans and purposes, Christians can come to a deeper and fuller knowledge of a heavenly Father. It can be like two people who love each other, though apart and unseen, yet through regular correspondence can keep in touch and grow closer together as they share their thoughts, experiences, prayers and plans. Fellowship begins with an introduction and grows to the fullest and most intimate communion with mind and heart. There must be the desire, a longing to know and the determination to work at this thing daily. To long for God, to worship, to seek, to taste, to touch with the heart, to see with the inner eye God's wonderful Person brings untold blessing to a believer. "Seek ye the Lord!"

> Dear Lord and Father of mankind,
> Forgive our foolish ways!
> Reclothe us in our rightful mind;

In purer lives Thy service find,
In deeper rev'rence, praise.

God is not only holy but He is love! (I John 4:8, 16). Perfect love is in Him. It is overflowing love. He created man to be the object of His love. "He first loved us." He loved and still loves the world of mankind (John 3:16).

God created man for His glory (Isaiah 43:7). He created man for His pleasure (Revelation 4:11). People mean something to God. They are valuable to Him—more valuable than precious jewels are to those who own and delight in them. God longs for a return of His love and a closeness of relationship with mankind. God wants to be valuable to His own. "Unto you therefore which believe he is precious [or valuable]" (I Peter 2:7).

What is the quality of God's love? It is longsuffering, it is kind, it is unselfish, it is patient, it is enduring, it never fails, it can be trusted, it is helpful and constructive, it loves truth and is eternal.

This love reaches out to the object of its affection, ever-seeking. A young man falls in love with a girl. She does not at first love him. He desires her and will not stop until he woos and wins her for himself. Sometimes he fails, for human love does not measure up to the love of God.

A young man in his early thirties was living a contented life in a new home with his wife and four children. He was interested in his good job, his full and satisfying life. Suddenly came a terrible jolt with the announcement of his wife that she was through with him and wanted no more to do with him. She wanted the home, the children, the car and his money, but she did not want him. The shock was shattering in every way. As the weeks went by nothing changed except a new experience with a living, loving God, who became real to him and helped him to find a love that was deep, real, and unfailing. The human love that he knew had disappointed and failed him, but God's love, filling his heart and mind, brought comfort and a joy he never before had known. The answer was God!

George Matheson was a young man very much in love with a girl who had promised to marry him. He looked forward to the day when they would be together. Suddenly he found that he was going hopelessly blind. He went to see her to tell her the news, thinking she loved him enough to marry him anyway. Instead she very coldly and finally told him she would not marry a blind man and broke the engagement. He went away heartbroken. The result of this heartbreak was recorded in this familiar hymn:

> O Love that wilt not let me go,
> I rest my weary soul in Thee;
> I give Thee back the life I owe,
> That in Thine ocean depths its flow
> May richer, fuller be.
>
> O Light that followest all my way,
> I yield my flickering torch to Thee;
> My heart restores its borrowed ray,
> That in Thy sunshine's blaze its day
> May brighter, fairer be.

God is Light! "In Him is no darkness at all" (I John 1:5). He produced light in the beginning—good light—and separated it from the darkness. Sin is dark. Christians have been "called" out of darkness into His marvelous light and are "now the people of God" (I Peter 2:9, 10). Therefore we are to walk in the light (I John 1:7).

Evil men love darkness rather than light, for most wicked deeds are carried out in the dark (John 3:19, 20, 21). "He that doeth truth cometh to the light." We Christians must continually come to the light and walk in it. "For ye were sometimes darkness, but now are ye light in the Lord: walk as children of light" (Ephesians 5:8). In other words, act like a child of God. As a small boy follows his father around and imitates his actions, mannerisms, and way of speaking because he loves and admires him, so we Christians should copy God's ways: "That ye may be blameless and harmless, the sons of God, without rebuke, in the midst of a crooked and perverse nation, among whom ye shine as lights in the world; Holding forth the word of life . . ." (Philippians 2:15, 16).

Jesus said, "Thou shalt love the Lord thy God with all thy heart, with all thy soul and with all thy strength and with all thy mind." To love a holy God this way will be to give ourselves over to Him—to have His love fill our hearts and His light to enlighten our minds.

To be a true friend of a loving, righteous God should be the aim of every Christian. "If any man love God, the same is known of him" (I Corinthians 8:3). God acknowledges this love.

Because God the Father is holy, is love, and is light, He had to act to bring His lost creation back to Himself. There was no way to do it except to send "His Son," the second Person of the Trinity, to earth as a human being. In the tenth chapter of Hebrews an account is given in verses 5-7 of a conversation in heaven when God the Son speaks to God the Father. The Son says, "For it is not possible that the blood of bulls and of goats should take away sins . . . . Sacrifice and offering thou wouldest not, but a body hast thou prepared me: In burnt offerings and sacrifices for sin thou hast had no pleasure. Then said I, Lo, I come . . . to do thy will, O God."

No creation of God except that of a human being could take away man's sins. Jesus became the "Sacrificial Offering."

> There was no other good enough
> To pay the price of sin;
> He only could unlock the gate
> Of heaven and let us in.

In Hebrews 9:22 we read: "Without shedding of blood is no remission [of sin]." "Neither by the blood of goats and calves, but by his own blood he entered in once into the holy place, having obtained eternal redemption for us" (Hebrews 9:12).

"But when the fulness of the time was come God sent forth his Son, made of a woman" (Galatians 4:4). The Son had a God-made body conceived by the Holy Ghost (Spirit)—a human body with blood in it—a body that was broken on the cross and the blood spilled out for the sins of the world.

Jesus is the Savior of mankind, the only one able to save all who come unto God by Him. This salvation means complete deliverance from sin—past, present, and future—for each person who accepts it. The only way a person can become good is by receiving Christ, the righteous one, into his life by faith.

A much loved father of nine children in the Kentucky Mountains was not a Christian at sixty-seven years of age. He had been a subject of prayer for years since his oldest daughter had been saved through the ministry of Christian workers in the community.

All the prayers, the efforts to tell him in words, his reading of the Bible, had been in vain; and it looked hopeless apart from faith in God's promises. The words that had encouraged continued prayer were found in James 4:2: "Ye have not because ye ask not."

The answer came most unexpectedly and through most difficult circumstances. Sudden illness made it necessary for the father to be hospitalized with pneumonia and a heart condition. Great concern was felt by all his family and much prayer was made, not just for his recovery but for his salvation.

A godly missionary who knew his Bible and knew how to talk to mountain people visited the sick man in the hospital and told him that the way to be saved was by grace through faith in the Lord Jesus Christ. He had prayer with him but no decision was made. Later on the father said he understood what was said, but it looked too easy.

After ten days in the hospital he was well enough to go home, but a month later he became sick again and had to return to the same hospital. This time the answer came. On Sunday morning the patient suddenly asked a daughter who was with him to get a preacher. To the young man who came he made his profession of faith and received the Lord Jesus Christ as his personal Savior.

A little later he said to the daughter, "Do you believe Jesus can save a man's soul?" When she replied, "Yes, Dad, I know He can," he said, "I know He can too, because He just saved me. He's in my heart!" Then he told her that for the first time in his life that morning he had seen himself as a sinner, and the prettiest picture he had ever seen was Jesus dying on the cross for him.

He got much worse; and the doctors, though they thought he could not live, worked hard to do all they could for him with blood transfusions and intravenous feeding. A daughter-in-law noticed some bleeding, which fact led to the discovery that he had a bleeding ulcer. A strict diet and proper care, with the Lord's help, brought him through.

To his oldest daughter he said, "I love you children better than anything in the world. They are doing everything they can here for me, but I wish they'd have let me go home" and pointed his finger upward. Another day when his faithful wife came to see him, his face all lighted up and he said, "Aren't you going to hug me?" She went to the bed, put her arms around him, and gave him a good hug while he patted her on the back. This was more affection than he usually showed before others.

He made a miraculous recovery and returned home in a short time. Just as soon as he was strong enough, he wanted to be baptized in the creek near his home. When the preacher asked him if he believed Jesus Christ was the Son of God, the Savior of the world, he replied, "I not only believe that; I know He is. He's in my heart!"

To his family and friends gathered around, he gave a clear testimony of his new-found faith in Christ and said he should have done this thirty years ago. His daughter commented, "No one was praying for him thirty years ago." One of his neighbors who belonged to the "Jesus Only" religion that denies the triune God, asked him one day if he believed in just one or in three Persons. His answer was very positive: "I believe just what the Bible says—three Persons."

When I visited him in his home one day, he told of the fine care he had received from the doctor and nurses; but the ringing words that thrilled me were these: "With all their good care of me it was my Lord who brought me through."

The most striking change in his life was evident to his family and neighbors. It had been a habit from childhood to use the name of the Lord in vain, emphasizing and punctuating his sentences with God's name. No one could persuade him it was wrong. His wife testified that from the day he was saved until his death she never heard him once use the Lord's name except in love and honor. He had indeed become a new creature in Christ Jesus. Old things had passed away. All things had become new.

Christ is not only Savior but He is Lord. A lord is a person having great power and authority, a ruler, a master. He speaks and expects to be obeyed. Jesus said, "Ye call me Lord, Lord and do not the things which I say." The wise man who builds his house on a rock is the one who does what Jesus says.

A Christian's body is for the Lord and is to be presented to Him as a living sacrifice, not to be used as he pleases but as God chooses (Romans 12:1). He should give himself unreservedly to Christ, his Master. He must glorify God in his body, for he was "bought with a price [the blood of Christ]" (I Corinthians 6:20). A Christian has no right to his own life.

When I was a young missionary in the Kentucky Mountains years ago, when travel was by horseback, muleback, jolt wagon, or on foot, I bought the first horse I ever owned. He was a large, rawboned, surefooted animal named Fred. I needed him to take me up creeks, over mountains, through rivers, and up and down rough roads to reach the people with the Word of God.

He was very hard to control, but because he was mine—I had paid a good price for him—I determined I would teach him that I was his owner and he must obey me.

I can still see myself with a bridle in hand, opening the gate to the lot where he was running free for exercise. As soon as I was inside the gate I turned and quickly fastened it, barring his escape. Then he did his best to scare and bluff me by running and plunging at me, laying his ears back and doing everything possible to keep me from catching and bridling him.

It took a few weeks of patient working with Fred, talking to him, standing my ground, waving him away from me when he charged me, to convince him that I was his boss. From then on he was my friend and docile as a lamb. He seemed to love me and want to obey me. He was willing to yield to the drawing of the reins to start, to go right, left, straight ahead, or to stop at my command. This was control with love—a working combination. After that we spent many happy hours together riding through the mountains to make Christ known in homes, in Sunday schools, or wherever possible.

Jesus wants His own to be His servants to do God's work in God's way in the world. Paul, James, John, Peter, and Jude called themselves the servants of Jesus Christ. It took training, self-denial, yieldedness of body, the renewing of their minds to know and do the perfect will of God. In dangerous situations Paul found guidance and protection from his Lord. In Corinth the Lord came to Paul in a vision in the night and told him not to be afraid, but to speak and be bold for He was with him; no one would hurt him; there were many people in the city who would become Christians. Paul believed and obeyed his Master and stayed in Corinth for a year and a half teaching the Word of God. As a result a church was established in that city.

How should we Christians act toward the second Person of the Trinity? We should obey His commands "straightway," "immediately." Peter and Andrew left their nets straightway and "followed

Him." At the marriage at Cana, Jesus' mother said to the servants, "Whatsoever he saith unto you, do it." They obeyed Him immediately and a miracle was performed that brought blessing, great wonder, and belief in Him.

Jesus told His disciples in John 14:21, "He that hath my commandments and keepeth them, he it is that loveth me . . . and I will love him and manifest myself to him." To know Him we must obey Him.

> Fairest Lord Jesus! Ruler of all nature!
> O, Thou of God and man the Son!
> Thee will I cherish, Thee will I honor,
> Thou, my soul's glory, joy and crown!

The Lord Jesus stayed down here only thirty-three and a half years. When He knew the time was approaching for Him to return to His Father, He called His disciples together. He told them He was leaving them but would pray the Father to send another Comforter (Helper) to be with them forever.

In verses in John 14, 15, and 16, Jesus spoke of the third Person of the Godhead, the Holy Spirit. Here He called Him "the Comforter," "He," "Him," "the Spirit of truth," "the Holy Ghost." Jesus said the Comforter would be in them, would teach them all things; would remind them of His spoken words, would testify of Christ, would reprove or convict of sin, would show them things to come, and would glorify Jesus Christ and take the things of Christ and show them to the disciples.

Here is a Person, not an influence. He is a Person who is love. He can be "grieved" (Ephesians 4:30). He is a Person who has power. His power can be "quenched" (I Thessalonians 5:19) like a fire, extinguished, smothered, or dampened. He is a Person who leads God's children (Romans 8:14). He helps Christians to know how to pray (Romans 8:26). He reveals the deep things of God to a believer (I Corinthians 2:10). He gives the spirit of revelation in the knowledge of Christ (Ephesians 1:17). He strengthens a believer in the inner man (Ephesians 3:16). He fills or controls a Christian who is obedient to God's command: "Be filled with the Spirit" (Ephesians 5:18). He gives gifts to believers (Hebrews 2:4). He is not "the spirit of fear, but of power and of love and of a sound mind" (II Timothy 1:7).

How then are we to act toward this wonderful Person who is in us? First of all, we must recognize His presence. We must let Him lead and guide us. We must let Him reveal the truth of God and of Christ in the Bible. We must let the Holy Spirit be our teacher of spiritual things. We must let the Spirit of God reveal sin in our lives. We must let the Spirit of God teach us the things concerning the future. We must be careful not to grieve the Holy Spirit by lack of love or disobedience or to quench His power by ignoring Him and throwing cold water on His plans. We must depend upon the Holy Spirit to tell us what we should pray for. The indwelling Spirit will give us wisdom, knowledge, strength, spiritual gifts, power, love, and a sound mind (the mind of Christ) if we will meet the requirements which are faith, obedience, and yieldedness.

The command of God is "Be filled with the Spirit." To obey this command, we must first want to be Spirit-filled. Then we must ask God to cleanse us from all sin. Then we must yield ourselves to God and let the indwelling Spirit fill us with Himself, the Spirit of love—perfect love, "all other loves excelling." There is then produced a life that is constantly in tune with God, a life that is obeying the Master, the Lord Jesus, and a life that is in reality enjoying "the communion of the Holy Spirit." Then we can fully "glorify God and enjoy Him forever"—now and always.

> Spirit of God, descend upon my heart;
> Wean it from earth, through all its pulses move;
> Stoop to my weakness, mighty as Thou art,
> And make me love Thee as I ought to love.
>
> Hast Thou not bid us love Thee, God and King?
> All, all Thine own, soul, heart and strength and mind;
> I see Thy cross—there teach my hand to cling:
> O let me seek Thee, and O let me find.
>
> Teach me to love Thee as Thine angels love,
> One holy passion filling all my frame;
> The baptism of the heav'n-descended Dove,
> My heart an altar, and Thy love the flame.

CHAPTER THREE

Toward

Ourselves—God's Workmanship

For we are His workmanship [His handiwork, formed by His hands], created in Christ Jesus unto good works, which God hath before ordained that we should walk in them" (Ephesians 2:10).

Christians are those of us who have become new creatures in Christ Jesus by the regenerating power of the Holy Spirit on God's part and an act of faith on our part. The first thing we must do is to examine ourselves to know whether Jesus Christ is in us (II Corinthians 13:5). If we are honest about this, the Holy Spirit will witness with our human spirits that we are the children of God (Romans 8:16).

Each of us is an individual person. Just as there are no two snowflakes alike, no two fingerprints alike, no two sets of human teeth alike (according to a dentist), and no two known human bodies with the same chemistry, so there are no two personalities exactly alike, even in identical twins. God has made us that way. We are ourselves—God's masterpiece, His highest form of creation.

We know that God made a man with a body and breathed His life into that body, giving Adam a never-dying soul and a spirit with which he could worship God.

In this chapter we want to recognize the soul as the person God has made us—that which we really are—with emotion, intellect, and a free will. The only creature to which He gave a free will is man.

What do we mean by "soul"? It is sometimes said, "She's a good old soul" or "She's a patient soul" or "He's a courageous soul" or "He's a good guy." The expressions mean the same: a good, patient, or courageous person—that which he or she really is.

The purpose of this chapter is to see how we as Christians should act toward this self of ours so that others will recognize that we belong to Jesus Christ.

A small boy giving his testimony over the radio one Saturday morning said something like this: "I was raised up where there were no Christians. My mother became a Christian and took me with her to a meeting. I wanted to go along because I had never been around a bunch of Christians before. I watched to see how they acted. Then I decided to become a Christian." We do not know what the boy saw in those people, but it must have been some likeness to Jesus Christ.

A beautiful but non-fragrant plant was delivered to a home from a florist shop. To the surprise of the lady who received it, the plant had the delicious, pungent fragrance of heliotrope. In a few days the odor disappeared entirely. It seemed to be such a strange thing that the florist was contacted. The conclusion was reached that the gift plant had been placed next to a heliotrope plant in the greenhouse, where it had absorbed its wonderful fragrance. Separated from the heliotrope, the odorless plant gradually lost the lovely perfume and returned to its natural state.

This is an excellent illustration of what was recognized by the Jewish rulers in Jerusalem (Acts 4:13) when they saw the boldness of Peter and John, perceived they were unlearned and ignorant men, marvelled and "took knowledge of them that they had been with Jesus." There was only one possible explanation: Peter and John were changed men. They were no longer simple fishermen but Spirit-filled followers of Jesus Christ. They had absorbed His fragrance. His presence in them had changed their lives. Staying close to Jesus kept them continually different from their old selves.

> Thou, my everlasting portion, more than friend or life to me;
> All along my pilgrim journey, Saviour, let me walk with Thee.
> Close to Thee, close to Thee, close to Thee, close to Thee;
> All along my pilgrim journey, Saviour, let me walk with Thee.

As individuals probably the first thing we become aware of is our bodies. We spend a lot of time, thought, and money on these bodies. They are important to God and to us. "The body is . . . for the Lord; and the Lord for the body" (I Corinthians 6:13). He wants to fill us with Himself.

God wants us to present our bodies to Him—"a living sacrifice" (Romans 12:1), to give them to Him completely and continually. These bodies have been bought with a price—"the precious [valuable] blood of Jesus"—and are not our own. They are the temples or dwelling places of the Holy Spirit, who is within, and we are to "glorify God" in our bodies, which belong to Him (I Corinthians 6:19, 20). "We have this treasure [the light of the knowledge of the glory of God in the face of Jesus Christ] in earthen vessels, that the excellency of the power may be of God and not of us" (II Corinthians 4:6, 7). Paul stated in Philippians 1:20 that his desire was to have Christ magnified in his body. In other words, Paul wanted the living Lord Jesus Christ to be important in his body. He said, "Christ liveth in me."

If we make Christ important in our bodies, then we cannot use these bodies for selfish, sinful purposes. The word "flesh" is used many times in the New Testament and often refers to the self life. If we take off the "h" and spell the word backwards, what do we have? "S E L F."

These bodies have many members: eyes, ears, a mouth, a nose, hands, feet, and various organs that keep us functioning in daily life. The body "is fearfully and wonderfully made" and is the vehicle in which God moves or gets around on earth. People get around physically on foot, by car, by plane, train, boat, bus, space ship, or other means of transportation to attend to their business. God uses human bodies to accomplish His business on earth. He has said, "I will dwell in them and walk in them" (II Corinthians 6:16). We are His transportation. It is important that we keep our bodies in good condition, as we would a car, boat, or plane. Who wants to fly on a plane or ride in a bus that is in poor condition?

Daniel in the Old Testament kept his body in excellent shape and would not eat the king's food or drink the king's wine that he knew would not be good for him. Instead he asked for a simple diet of vegetables and water. As a result he looked much better than the young men who ate the king's food and drank the wine. He was accepted and used mightily in the kingdom.

Our bodies must be disciplined if we are to live for God in running the race of life.

Paul said, "I keep under my body, and bring it into subjection" (I Corinthians 9:27). He hardened, punished, and trained his body to be what it should be, just as an athlete trains in order to win a game or a fight. For a Christian, life is a game or life is a fight. "Endure hardness as a good soldier of Jesus Christ" (II Timothy 2:3).

> Fight the good fight with all thy might!
> Christ is thy strength, and Christ thy right;
> Lay hold on life, and it shall be
> Thy joy and crown eternally.

We are told to "mortify" our members and to count as dead the sinful things of earth—sins of the body, evil desires. The news media today are full of accounts of young people and others who are mistreating and wrecking their bodies through promiscuous sex, drink, drugs, and wild living, giving their bodies over to everything that weakens and wrecks rather than to God, who strengthens and delivers.

Sex sins top the lists in several New Testament passages, where we are told what not to do: Mark 7:21, Romans 1:26-29, Ephesians 5:3, and Colossians 3:5.

We have members of our bodies through which desires come: eyes, ears, mouth, nose, and hands. God gives us five senses— seeing, hearing, tasting, smelling, and feeling—to respond to the highest and best in life, not to the lowest and basest.

A twelve-year-old boy in a Bible class at our summer camp was discussing with me, his teacher, the subject of the two natures in a Christian: the old nature and the new nature. He said he was a Christian and often had trouble with himself. Chocolate candy, for instance, was a favorite of his. His mother frequently made chocolate fudge while cooking dinner. She cut it up in squares, put it in a dish on the dining room table, and always told him not to eat even one piece until after dinner because it would spoil his appetite. Sometimes he obeyed and sometimes he slipped into the dining room while she was in the kitchen and took one or two pieces.

Why did he act that way? The candy smelled delicious (his nose), it looked so good (his eyes), he knew it would have a wonderful taste (his mouth), he heard his mother say, "Don't touch" and Satan say, "Go ahead; she'll never know" (his ears); but his old selfish nature said, "I want some," and he reached for and took the candy (his hand). He sinned with his five members because he chose to. He disobeyed God because he disobeyed his mother, for the Bible says, "Children, obey your parents in the Lord" (Ephesians 6:1). He yielded to his own desires. The old nature won, and the boy displayed weakness rather than strength. "Neither yield ye your members as instruments of unrighteousness unto sin: but yield yourselves unto God, . . . and your members as instruments of righteousness unto God" (Romans 6:13).

From more recent news about this same boy I learned that he evidently did not train himself to say "No" to bodily temptation, for at college he became involved with the wrong girl and spoiled his life. It would have paid him to do like Joseph, a young man in the Bible who knew what was right and did it. He had trained his senses "to discern both good and evil" (Hebrews 5:14).

The apostle Paul had trouble with himself. In Romans 7:15-25 he wrote words to this effect: "I want to do the right thing and do it not. I do what I hate. I want to do good, but I do evil instead. O wretched man that I am, who shall deliver me from this deadly lower nature of mine [the old, sinful, carnal nature that he was born with]?" Twenty-six times in eleven verses he used the pronoun "I." Seven times he used "me" and four times he said "my." He found he could not deliver himself from this selfish nature he had received from Adam through his parents. The answer was found in Jesus Christ, his Lord, who lived, as a man, a life of victory over every form of bodily temptation.

A young girl who was near suicide, looking for happiness in drugs, liquor, free love, and worldly pleasures, went to a Bible study out of curiosity. She became seriously interested. After she had searched and studied the Scriptures for months, John 3:16 spoke to her heart and she received Christ as her Savior and gave her life to Him. She had never known such happiness could exist. She said, "Jesus Christ blows your mind. God shows you how to love and what it feels like to be loved." He was what she had been looking for since her early teens. He was "the bag" she had not found. She thought that trying things and bumming around the country would make her free; but they were all traps. Sin was the trap that led her to confusion, unhappiness, and guilt. Christ made her free! "If the Son therefore shall make you free, ye shall be free indeed" (John 8:36). She found that being a Christian was exciting, "because there's always a new challenge." When she sees past friends, instead of talking about drugs and clothes and what is happening on the scene, she now tells them what is really happening with God. He has made her new.

Take my life, and let it be consecrated, Lord, to Thee.
Take my hands . . . my feet . . . . my voice . . . . my will . . . .
my heart . . . . for Thee.

In Romans 12:2, after being told in verse 1 to present our bodies to God, we are told to be transformed by the renewing of our minds. In these bodies of ours we have God-given minds. We are to change our minds and let them be remade with new thoughts and attitudes so we will not go our own way but will go God's way. The right motive and the right attitude are most important in enabling us to live a successful Christian life according to the will of God. We need to check ourselves constantly with "why?" and "how?" in all our actions and words. With our renewed minds we can prove what is the good and acceptable and perfect will of God. "Wherefore be ye not unwise, but understanding what the will of the Lord is" (Ephesians 5:17).

We are to be transformed mentally from the standard thinking of the world around us by letting God completely change our minds to know His standards in order to do His will and think His way. "Let this mind be in you, which was also in Christ Jesus" (Philippians 2:5). In the last part of I Corinthians 2:16, we read: "But we have the mind of Christ." In II Timothy 1:7, we find that God has given us believers "a sound mind." Surely that sound mind is the mind of the Lord Jesus Christ, who perfectly did the will of God.

Every Christian is born of the Spirit and has a spiritual nature, but every Christian is not spiritually minded. Paul said to the Corinthian Christians, "Ye are yet carnal . . . there is among you envying and strife and divisions . . . ye . . . walk as men" (I Corinthians 3:3).

Jesus hated sin; so must we. Jesus emptied Himself and made Himself of no reputation. Jesus wanted the Father's will and did it. Jesus showed mercy and forgiveness to His enemies. This is the mind of Christ as revealed in the Scriptures.

With our minds we are told to think about what is true, honest, just, pure, lovely, and of good report (Philippians 4:8). In other words, we must use our minds or train them to think about good things, fine things, clean things, lovely things, and good news about others. It is hard today not to get disgusted with the evil things and reports of bad things about people and pass on the news we hear. We can become callous to these reports and accept the present sins as a way of life.

Jesus lived in the midst of evil actions and evil reports. He did not dwell on and gossip about these, but denounced the evil and the evil doers. He spoke God's truth, which had an effect on sinful lives. Some people believed on Him and were changed, whereas His enemies hated, persecuted, and finally killed Him.

Daniel in the Old Testament not only disciplined his body but turned his mind over to God and allowed Him to give him "knowledge and skill in all learning and wisdom." As a result, King Nebuchadnezzar of Babylon found Daniel ten times better in wisdom and understanding than all the magicians and astrologers that were in all his realm (Daniel 1:17, 20).

This is what God will do with any of us who will yield our minds to Him continually. This is what Paul prayed for the Christians in Colossians 1:9 and 10: "that ye might be filled with the knowledge of his will in all wisdom and spiritual understanding; That ye might walk worthy of the Lord unto all pleasing, being fruitful in every good work, and increasing in the knowledge of God."

If we practice having the mind of Christ in all things, we will find our minds sharpened, enlightened, delighted, and filled with good and constructive thoughts which can be passed on to others by spoken or written word. This kind of mind will cause our daily lives to be a joy to us and a blessing to others. This is an exciting way to live.

Another part of us which is of daily importance is our hearts—our inmost feeling. Someone has said, "When the mind of Christ is developed in us, we also will love God with our total being as Jesus did." God is overflowing love. In Colossians 3:2 we are told to set our "affection on things above," heavenly things. Our minds and our hearts work together in this act. In chapter 3, verse 14, Paul says, "Above all . . . put on charity [love]." Again our minds must act. Love should run our lives.

A motorist driving west saw two young fellows standing beside a car on the highway. He stopped to ask whether they needed help. They told him they would appreciate it if he would push the car down the highway. He agreed and pushed it quite a distance until they came to some filling stations. After passing the second station, he stopped, got out of his car, and asked the young men why they had not gone into one of the stations for gas. One fellow replied, "Well, you see, sir, this car has no engine. We thought we'd see how far we could get across the country by being pushed, and we've already gone five hundred miles." There was no power from within to run that car. Other cars were running it. So many Christians are like that—allowing other people to push them through life rather than letting God do it from within. Love is power! In Romans 5:5 we read that "the love of God is shed abroad in our hearts by the Holy Ghost [Spirit] which is given unto us." Every Christian has the love of God in him, a power that can move him moment by moment in God's way if he will let it.

> Moment by moment I'm kept in His love;
> Moment by moment I've life from above;
> Looking to Jesus till glory doth shine;
> Moment by moment, O Lord, I am thine.

Jesus said the greatest commandment of all was to "love the Lord thy God with all thy heart." Daniel must have loved God with all his heart to give Him the glory in interpreting impossible dreams, to pray when he was threatened with the lions' den, and to endeavor to be the right kind of Jew, who worshipped only the living God.

God is not mentioned in the book of Esther; but it is evident that Esther, her cousin Mordecai, and other Jews in the palace at Shushan trusted and loved God and their own nation, or there would not have been fasting (which meant praying also) for deliverance from an impossible situation. It took great faith, courage, and love for Esther to risk her life to save God's chosen people.

Daniel and Esther were both strong in body and in mind with hearts of love that changed the course of history. They were well-behaved, respected young people. What they did was not easy. They did not love themselves first.

36

Purer yet and purer I would be in mind,
Dearer yet and dearer every duty find;
Hoping still and trusting God without a fear,
Patiently believing He will make all clear.

Calmer yet and calmer in the hour of pain,
Surer yet and surer peace at last to gain;
Suff'ring still and doing, to His will resigned,
And to God subduing heart, and will and mind.

"Now the end of the commandment is charity [love] out of a pure heart" (I Timothy 1:5). "Blessed are the pure in heart for they shall see God" (Matthew 5:8). How marvelous to be able to see the Lord in all His majesty because our hearts are pure. Peter writes to believers, "I stir up your pure minds by way of remembrance" (II Peter 3:1).

What is it to be "pure" in heart and mind? The dictionary gives us a choice of several definitions: "clear, cleansed, unmixed, free from sin or guilt." Perhaps the words we want here are "cleansed" and "unmixed." If we have a glass of clear, pure water in our hand it is free from pollution (usually by chlorination) and is healthful and refreshing to drink. Suppose a friend comes along with a pitcher of milk and jokingly pours a little milk into our glass. What happens? The water becomes mixed and is no longer clear, palatable, or refreshing. It is no longer pure.

This is what happens to Christians when they allow self, something, or someone else to take God's place in their lives. Whatever replaces God first in our affections becomes an idol; and John said, "Little children, keep yourselves from idols" (I John 5: 21). We have the mind of Christ; so let us yield to Him and love God with all our hearts and minds, with a genuine love from our whole being.

Two hands for His service;
One tongue for His praise;
Two feet to run for Him
And walk in His ways;
Two eyes to gaze on Him;
Two ears Him to hear;
One heart for Him only,
Each day of the year.

37

We just naturally love ourselves. If we have a picture taken with a group, whose picture do we look for first? Our own, of course, and if we do not like it, the group picture is no good.

Someone has said: "There are three you's: (1) the person you think you are; (2) the person others think you are; (3) the person God knows you are and can be through Christ." God loves us and wants us just as we are to mold and make us in the image of His Son (II Corinthians 3:18). He wants us to "grow up into . . . Christ" (Ephesians 4:15). Our task is to let Christ transform us, to count on Him to act as a Person in us. Knowing Christ as a Person changes things in our lives, our standards to His standards. A Christian's standards have to flow from the heart.

Just as soon as we determine that we want to please God and give our bodies, our minds, and our hearts to Him in submission for His will to be done in us, trouble comes as it did to Paul. The old "I" we were born with—the old nature, the old man, the self-life—objects, wants to be independent of God's control (for that is what sin is); and a battle is on. There is conflict within; "the flesh lusteth against the Spirit and the Spirit against the flesh; and these are contrary the one to the other, so that ye cannot do the things that ye would" (Galatians 5:17).

The self-life is strong and evil. Not only are sex sins on the lists in the New Testament but also named in up-to-date language are the following: evil thoughts, hatred, bad temper, drunkenness, pride, murder, envy, thefts, covetousness, quarreling, greed, deceit, haughtiness, slander, arrogance, folly, foolishness, spiritism, fighting, complaints, criticism, wild parties, constant effort to get the best for oneself and the feeling that everyone else is wrong except those in one's own little group. None of us can say we are guiltless of all these sins and be honest. Pride is named with murder, bad temper with adultery, coveting with drunkenness, and so on.

In these days of so much sex sin, so much drug addiction, and so much covetousness, we have also so much drunkenness. In the New Testament we have such verses as Luke 21:34, Romans 13:13, Romans 14:21, I Corinthians 5:11, I Corinthians 6:10, Galatians 5:21, Ephesians 5:18, and I Thessalonians 5:7, 8, where we are told about drunkenness: "and take heed to yourselves lest at any time your hearts be overcharged with . . . drunkenness"; "Let us walk honestly as in the day not . . . in drunkenness"; "It is good neither . . . to drink wine . . . whereby thy brother stumbleth, or is offended or is made weak"; "not to keep company . . . [with] a drunkard"; "[drunkards] . . . shall not inherit the kingdom of God"; "be not drunk with wine"; and "they that be drunken are drunken in the night."

Instead of getting drunk, what are Christians to do from the context of these verses? They are to "watch . . . and pray always"; to "put . . . on the Lord Jesus Christ, and make not provision for the flesh to fulfil the lusts thereof"; to "follow after the things which make for peace, and things wherewith one may edify another"; to "put away from among themselves that wicked person"; not "to be brought under the power of any of the things that are lawful for them . . . "; to "walk in the Spirit, and . . . not fulfil the lust of the flesh"; to "be filled with the Spirit"; and finally to "be sober, putting on the breastplate of faith and love."

What can we do about ourselves and our tendency to express self rather than Jesus Christ? Jesus provided for our need for victory when He died on the cross. When He cried, "It is finished," He knew He had paid the full price for our sins. In Him we can conquer our sinful selves if we want to. Dr. Billy Graham has been reported as saying that ninety-five percent of all Christians are defeated. They are living in guilt, succumbing to sin because they have lost their ability to resist temptation. Sin in Christians should be recognized and confessed. All confessed sin will never be brought to judgment.

Paul says a great deal about "ourselves" in II Corinthians. We are not to "trust in ourselves but in God" (1:9); we are not "sufficient of ourselves to think anything as of ourselves" (3:5); by manifesting the truth we should be "commending ourselves to every man's conscience in the sight of God" (4:2); we should "preach not ourselves but Christ Jesus the Lord" (4:5); we should be " in all things approving ourselves as the ministers [servants] of God" (6:4); we should " cleanse ourselves from all filthiness of the flesh and spirit" (7:1); and " we dare not . . . compare ourselves" or measure ourselves with others (10:12). In II Thessalonians 3:6, 7 we read: "Now we command you . . . that ye withdraw yourselves from every brother that walketh disorderly . . . for we behaved not ourselves disorderly among you." We are to watch our companions because we are influenced by them and identified with them. We are to judge ourselves in the light of Christ's perfection (I Corinthians 11:31).

What are some of the wrong things Christians do? We justify rather than judge ourselves (very easy to do). We indulge, not discipline, ourselves. We pity ourselves rather than accept God's chastening which is for our good. We trust ourselves rather than God. We love ourselves instead of Jesus Christ. We love our own way, not His. We do not want the way of the cross, and yet Jesus said, "Deny thyself, take up thy cross and follow me." The cross means death to self, the whole person. Jesus also said, "He that loveth his life shall lose it," but we do not want to lose it in order to find it.

A Christian worker once said, "I know the cross means "I" crossed out; but there are some things I want to hang on to." He did, with the result that he failed as a Christian in character, fruitfulness, and example.

It is dangerous not to yield the whole person—body, soul, and spirit—to the Lord Jesus Christ. We must die to self and live for Him. It is not easy, but it works!

"I am crucified with Christ; nevertheless I live; yet not I, but Christ liveth in me; and the life which I now live in the flesh I live by the faith of the Son of God, who loved me, and gave himself for me" (Galatians 2:20).

> Dying with Jesus, by death reckoned mine;
> Living with Jesus, a new life divine;
> Looking to Jesus till glory doth shine,
> Moment by moment, O Lord, I am Thine.

We must recognize the truth about ourselves from the Bible, God's Word, and must want the victory over sin in our lives. That means we will take it by faith from the Lord Jesus Christ. He gives, I take the victory.

We must know how to pray to God so that our prayers are answered. That means real prayer—unselfish, believing, persistent, fervent, effectual praying that only the Holy Spirit can help us with. He, the Holy Spirit, "helpeth our infirmities" when we do not know what we ought to pray for (Romans 8:26). If we are right with God we can pray with confidence. "Beloved, if our heart condemn us not, then have we confidence toward God. And whatsoever we ask we receive of Him because we keep his commandments and do those things that are pleasing in his sight"

(I John 3:21, 22). There is no greater joy than to see Almighty God answer prayer because we love, obey, and want to please Him.

When we pray, we ought to believe God with genuine faith, defy doubt, be joyful in the Lord. Joy defeats Satan. We ought to have habitual contact with God—start the day by turning our hearts and minds to Christ, get our spirits in tune with Him, and be happy in Him. We ought to commit the day to Him and walk through it with Him in His way, not ours. As we do this we will know Him better each day. His love in us and our love for Him will set us free from ourselves.

We can trust ourselves only when we are in the center of the will of God. Then we have poise that no cultural training can give.

"As ye have therefore received Christ Jesus the Lord, so walk ye in him" (Colossians 2:6). This means taking one step at a time in each moment of life whether that step means life or death. In Revelation 12:11 there are those who "loved not their lives unto the death."

If we are Spirit-filled Christians we will be our very best selves—not a disappointment to God, to others, or to ourselves. We will find our true selves.

Not long ago a friend who knew me when I was a teen-ager said, "I can't get over the changed person you are from our days together in boarding school." She knew I was a timid, insecure introvert, with no initiative or any special interest or talents.

My answer to her was something like this: "Well, I gave myself unreservedly to the Lord, and He has made me what He wanted me to be—a fulfilled personality, able to do things for Him that I could never do without Him."

People are looking for genuine Christians, those who are "for real." It is not just our appearance that counts, although that is important. God looks on our hearts and others look for some likeness to Christ in us.

One day I was having a dress fitted in a local dress shop by a good fitter, a very nice person and a friend of mine. We were talking about how attractive it was to have people be pleasant to us rather than unpleasant. All sorts of women go to this specialty shop to buy clothes and in time reveal to those trying to help them what kind of persons they really are by the way they act. My fitter friend told of a former customer who was so hard to please,

41

so unpleasant and so rude every time she came into the shop that everyone who had any dealings with her was glad when she stopped coming. Then she made this remark: "What about a woman acting like that and quoting Bible verses to make us believe she was a good Christian?"

We need a revival of the individual, not to be like peas in a pod, all alike, trying to copy one another. Our example is Jesus Christ. In other words, we need to BE Christians. It is not just what we do that is important, but what we are.

The verse at the head of this chapter told us that we were "created in Christ Jesus unto good works . . . that we should walk in them."

Where do we start the good works? Right in our homes, our schools, our businesses, our churches, our communities and wherever we go. Life is not static. Life is moving. We are moving. We shall do better or worse next week, next month, or next year. If we do not move forward, we shall move backward. We are to abide in Christ, walk in Christ to bring forth fruit, which is the character of Christ in us, and bear witness of Him (John 15:27).

We sing:

> Be like Jesus, this my song, in the home and in the throng,
> Be like Jesus all day long, I would be like Jesus. [2]

But if we do not want or try to act like Him, we are singing a lie.

Filled with the Spirit, controlled by the Spirit, we will be the persons God intended us to be—happy, confident, useful, and Christ-like. There will be no inferiority complex, which is, in reality, false pride or false humility. We are children of the King!

We can look toward life as an adventure, an opportunity and a wonderful future.

> If you want to be distressed, look within,
> If you want to be defeated, look back;
> If you want to be distracted, look around;
> If you want to be dismayed, look ahead;
> If you want to be delivered, look up,
> If you want to be delighted, look to Christ!

A group of young men at the Air Force Academy were discussing Christianity. Some were sneering and making caustic remarks about some people who called themselves Christians. Finally, one fellow defiantly said, "Just show me one real Christian." Without hesitation a young man called out the name of a popular cadet. There could be no argument, for this popular young man was an honor student, an outstanding athlete, a moral and upright young person who lived a consistent Christian life. Christ was exalted in him.

My father was ninety-four years of age when he died. A connection of our family, a successful businessman, flew from Ohio to Pennsylvania to be present with us at the funeral. When he came into the home before we left for the church, he walked up to me, shook my hand, and said, "Ruth, your father was the man most like Christ that I have ever known." I was surprised, but pleased. What nicer thing could have been said about Father. After the church service was over, in a church filled with people, one man said to another, "That is the best-lived life I've ever seen."

God was honored in Father's life and death, for as I sat in the front pew of the church looking at my father's form (his person had gone to heaven), I told the Lord I wanted my life to continue to its end lived only for the Lord Jesus Christ. Then, quietly, I dedicated myself anew to Him.

> Not I, but Christ, be honored, loved, exalted;
> Not I, but Christ, be seen, be known, be heard;
> Not I, but Christ, in every look and action
> Not I, but Christ, in every thought and word.

Our testimony for the Lord Jesus should be uppermost in every action and in every decision we make. We bear His name and should safeguard it.

A young man in Kentucky thought his uncle was the best Christian he knew. When he visited in his home there would always be a blessing said at the table and Bible reading and prayer held for morning devotions. One day the uncle and nephew were going somewhere together in a car. Another passenger had a can of beer, which he opened and passed around. The nephew was stunned when his uncle turned up the can and drank from it. From then on he had no confidence in that uncle's Christianity.

I would be true, for there are those who trust me;
I would be pure, for there are those who care;
I would be strong, for there is much to suffer;
I would be brave, for there is much to dare.

I would be prayerful through each busy moment;
I would be constantly in touch with God;
I would be tuned to hear His slightest whisper;
I would have faith to keep the path Christ trod.

A missionary in India was so dull mentally he could not learn the language. After a few years he decided it was hopeless and wanted to resign and go home. Some of his fellow missionaries petitioned their board not to let him go, for they said he had a better influence on the heathen than any of the other missionaries. One of the converts when asked, "What is it to be a Christian?" replied, "It is to be like Mr. _____," naming the good missionary. He was kept in India.

Not merely in the words you say
Not only in the deeds confessed
But in the most unconscious way is Christ expressed.

For me, 'twas not the truths you taught,
To you, so clear, to me so dim,
But when you came to me you brought a sense of Him.

And from your eyes, He beckons me,
And from your heart His love is shed;
'Til I lose sight of you, and see the Christ instead.

"To him that overcometh will I grant to sit with me in my throne ... " (Revelation 3:21).

Do we want to reign with Christ above and share all the joys of overcoming while we are on this planet? Then you and I must know ourselves, as God's Word reveals to us the kind of persons we naturally are, and enter into the liberating knowledge of Christ (Philippians 3:10).

You and I need to respond anew to words from an old, familiar invitation hymn and let Jesus Christ make us what we ought to be.

Just as I am, and waiting not
To rid my soul of one dark blot,
To Thee whose blood can cleanse each spot.

Just as I am, though tossed about
With many a conflict, many a doubt,
Fightings and fears within, without.

Just as I am, poor, wretched, blind;
Sight, riches, healing of the mind,
Yea, all I need in Thee I find.

Just as I am, Thou wilt receive,
Wilt welcome, pardon, cleanse, relieve,
Because Thy promise I believe,
O Lamb of God, I come.

CHAPTER FOUR

Toward

Others—God's Plan

When we as Christians are fully yielded to the Lord and are filled with the love of God, we cannot keep to ourselves the knowledge of the wonderful Person, Jesus Christ, and His saving power.

The world is full of "others" who need the Lord Jesus Christ. And who are these others? I believe they are any and all persons in every place and all nations.

Jesus said, "For even the Son of Man came not to be ministered unto, but to minister, and to give his life a ransom for many" (Mark 10:45).

Jesus told His disciples to serve Him by serving others, to go and teach all nations, "teaching them to observe all things whatsoever I have commanded you." He told them in Acts 1:8 to "be witnesses unto me both in Jerusalem, and in all Judea, and in Samaria, and unto the uttermost part of the earth." They were to start right where they were and reach out to the farthest part of their known world to tell the story of His love.

> Proclaim to every people, tongue and nation
> That God in Whom they live and move is love;
> Tell how He stooped to save His lost creation,
> And died on earth that man might live above.
>
> Publish glad tidings, tidings of peace;
> Tidings of Jesus, redemption and release.

This small group of eleven disciples obeyed Jesus' commands and by their preaching "turned the world upside down"

(Acts 17:6). They began in Jerusalem right where they were, as He had said, where the enemies of Christ were all around them. Peter was no longer afraid of "maids" (Matthew 26:69, 71), and "they that stood by" (verse 73) when he denied his Lord in Pilate's hall. On the day of Pentecost he stood up before a multitude of Jews, "devout men, out of every nation under heaven," and boldly preached Christ to them as their Messiah and Savior (Acts 2). He was supported by the presence of the other disciples, who also gave their witness of the wonderful works of God (Acts 2:11). As a result three thousand Jews "gladly received his [Peter's] word," joined the disciples, were baptized, and continued with them praising God. Here were the first "others."

Witnessing of Jesus to others is God's plan. There is no other way to reach them, for this is His program, chosen by Him to save those who are lost in sin. As soon as a person finds Christ, he or she invariably becomes concerned for immediate loved ones and close friends. This was true of Andrew, who had heard Jesus first, was convinced that He was the Messiah, hunted up his brother Simon Peter, and brought him to Jesus. The next day Jesus found Philip, who in turn found Nathanael. As a result Nathanael was convinced and said, "Rabbi, thou art the Son of God; thou art the King of Israel" (John 1:49).

Jesus had said to begin at Jerusalem, but He did not stop there. The disciples were also to witness in Judea (close by) and in Samaria (a little farther away) and then on to other parts of the earth.

The believers stayed together in Jerusalem having a wonderful time of fellowship with one another and the new converts until severe persecution came upon them and Stephen was stoned to death. This persecution caused many to leave the city. In Acts 8:4 we read: "Therefore they that were scattered abroad went everywhere preaching the word." The Lord used persecution to start some of them moving out of Jerusalem according to His plan.

Philip was one who went down to the city of Samaria, where the despised Samaritans lived. The Samaritans were people of mixed blood and were shunned by the Jews. Philip "preached Christ unto them," obeying what Jesus had said in Acts 1:8, " . . . be witnesses unto me . . . in Samaria." As a result the people "gave heed" and "there was great joy in that city" (Acts 8:8).

Then Philip was led to go to the desert, where he found the Ethiopian eunuch, a man of a different color, a different race and nation. When asked by the eunuch to explain the meaning of Isaiah 53:7, 8, Philip "preached unto him Jesus." The eunuch, "a man of great authority," the queen's treasurer, believed with all his heart, was baptized, and went on his way rejoicing. And so, because of Philip's obedience, a man of another tongue and race had the message of salvation to give to "others" on a different continent.

To the amazement and great fear of the disciples, Saul of Tarsus, the Jewish leader who was waging a campaign to kill all the Jews who believed in Jesus Christ, appeared in Jerusalem to tell them he also had become a disciple. They would not believe it until Barnabas, a trusted Christian, told the account of Saul's conversion and vouched for his sincerity. Here was an example of how to act toward others as Barnabas stood up and spoke out for Saul, his new brother in Christ.

Also Ananias, in Acts 9:10-17, a believer in Jesus, had to overcome his prejudice and fear when the Lord told him to go to Saul and put his hand on him that Saul might receive his sight and become an instrument in God's hand. What a privilege that was for Ananias to be the one to free Saul (one "other") for the great work God was going to do through him.

Then Peter was put to the supreme test of obedience. Brought up a strict Jew, he loathed all Gentiles as unclean persons. How disturbed and distressed he was when he saw a vision of unclean beasts descending in a vessel (like a knitted sheet) from heaven and heard the Lord say, "Rise, Peter; kill, and eat." He soon understood this meant that he was to go to a house in Caesarea to preach God's word to Cornelius, who was a Roman soldier, a Gentile, and to Cornelius' kinsmen and near friends. Peter obeyed and learned that "God is no respecter of persons: But in every nation he that feareth Him, and worketh righteousness, [believes in Christ in his heart] is accepted with him" (Acts 10:34, 35.)

As Peter preached the gospel that day, the Gentiles in Cornelius' house believed, received the Holy Spirit, and were baptized (Acts 10:44-48). Thus the door opened for Gentile believers to become members of the church of Jesus Christ along with Jewish believers; to be "made nigh by the blood of Christ," members "of the household of God" (Ephesians 2:13, 19).

To accomplish this, Peter had to be willing to obey God by going to these others, visiting with them and telling them the story of Jesus' death, burial, and resurrection from the dead.

Then to further and widen the ministry of preaching the gospel to every creature, the Holy Spirit in Acts 13:1, 2 told the fasting and praying disciples at Antioch to separate Barnabas and Saul unto Him "for the work whereunto I have called them."

Obeying Him, they started their first missionary journey to carry the good news of Jesus beyond Jerusalem, Judea, and Samaria "unto the uttermost part of the earth."

And what a story that was and is—to follow Paul through his experiences as the Lord had said to Ananias in Acts 9:15, 16: " . . . for he is a chosen vessel unto me, to bear my name before the Gentiles, and kings, and the children of Israel. For I will show him how great things he must suffer for my name's sake."

Often alone, and suffering many hardships, Paul learned the secret of walking with Jesus.

> O Master, let me walk with Thee
> In lowly paths of service free;
> Tell me Thy secret; help me bear
> The strain of toil, the fret of care.
>
> Help me the slow of heart to move
> By some clear, winning word of love;
> Teach me the wayward feet to stay,
> And guide them in the homeward way.
>
> Teach me Thy patience! Still with Thee
> In closer, dearer company,
> In work that keeps faith sweet and strong,
> In trust that triumphs over wrong.

We should follow Paul's example as recorded in Romans 1:16, "For I am not ashamed of the gospel of Christ: for it is the power of God unto salvation to everyone that believeth; to the Jew first, and also to the Greek [Gentiles]."

Later on in Galatians 2:8 he wrote: "For he that wrought [worked] effectually in Peter to the apostleship of the circumcision, the same was mighty in me to the Gentiles." Paul was the

50

special messenger to the Gentiles as Peter was to the Jews; and God worked mightily in him and through him. He found out that God's plan to reach others through a man worked.

The New Testament church grew rapidly into the spiritual body of Christ, a building in which God dwells, whose members, as stones in the walls, are both Jews and Gentiles who have received the Lord Jesus Christ as their personal Savior (I Corinthians 12: 12, 13; Ephesians 2:19-22).

As this took place the disciples could realize what Jesus meant when He said in John 10:16: "And other sheep [Gentiles] I have, which are not of this fold [Jews]: them also I must bring, and they shall hear my voice; and there shall be one fold, and one shepherd."

What of today? We are still in the days of the New Testament church. There are many more people to reach. Means of reaching them have increased through modern methods of communication, but the message is the same: "Christ died for our sins according to the scriptures; and that he was buried, and that he rose again the third day according to the scriptures" (I Corinthians 15:3, 4).

God still uses people to do His work in the world. As we read the book of Acts and the Epistles, we soon find out how hard it was for those early Christians to communicate Christ to heathen people in every part of the known world. And it is not any easier today; because it is the way of the cross, it is offensive to the natural man, and it is the message which Satan opposes.

In John 17:18 Jesus prayed thus for His followers: "As thou hast sent me into the world, even so have I also sent them into the world."

If we Christians today concentrate on winning only our families and close friends to Christ, we are not obedient. There are others in our own communities, in our own area, in difficult places where people would be considered beneath our notice socially or religiously, or in a nearby place (as "in Samaria") where there is mixed blood and mixed faith. We are to go to them (in some way) by person, prayer, or gift, and then on to countries which are foreign to us, where it would be even harder to tell the story of Jesus.

Through modern communications, such as radio and TV, and better educational opportunities, the means of making Christ known are greater, varied, and more challenging.

51

Who'll go and help this Shepherd kind,
Help Him the wandering ones to find?
Who'll bring the lost ones to the fold,
Where they'll be sheltered from the cold?
     Bring them in . . . from the fields of sin;
     Bring them in . . . bring the wandering ones to Jesus.

A secret of successful service is love for God and love for our fellowmen. This is what the world expects to see in a true Christian.

Jesus prayed in John 17:26, asking His Father "that the love wherewith thou hast loved me may be in them." That love is a love which is not selfish but reaches out to others. We need that love of God in our hearts, giving us warmth and concern if we are to serve Him in touching other lives. It is basic in our relation to others if we are to win them to Christ.

Recently Lew Alcindor, the star basketball player who graduated from U.C.L.A. in 1969, was quoted as saying: "The Bible had no further meaning for me. The Bible and its teachings had produced all these hate-filled people; it seemed to me that there was nothing in the world as unlike Christ as Christians!" What a tragedy!

Jesus gave a commandment to His disciples: "That ye love one another, as I have loved you." Christians are failures and are stumbling blocks if they do not obey this commandment in John 15:12. It was important enough for Jesus to repeat it in verse 17.

Something is radically wrong with Christian work today, in many cases causing failure to reach others for Jesus. This is reported from mission fields all over the world. The training or motive or attitude must be wrong.

A high-school senior was expelled with some other students from a Christian boarding school because of flagrant disobedience of rules. He blamed the teachers, but not the headmaster, for failing to show Christian love to the students. His heartbroken Christian father asked him what he wanted or expected to find in a Christian faculty. He answered, "I don't want to be looked upon as a project; I want to be looked upon as a person."

Two Christian mountaineers who are active for the Lord among their own people recently said about some missionaries who had come to their vicinity, "They come from nothing, they get two or three years of Bible training, they think they know it all, and they think they are better than we are and look down on us. Then they want us to be like them and (very emphatically) we don't want to be like them. We want to be ourselves as God intends us to be." These friends did not want to imitate something they did not like. They neither saw the beauty nor felt the love of Christ and His humility in those missionaries. The Bible tells us, " . . . in lowliness of mind let each esteem other better than themselves."

Jesus set us an example of humble service when He, the King of Glory, stooped to wash the disciples' feet. He said they should do as He had done. His motive was love and His attitude was not condescension but humility. He was "the meek and lowly Jesus." This combination of love and humility should be one of our first qualifications for Christian service.

Jesus said we were to love our neighbor as ourselves. He said we should do to others as we would want them to do to us. This Jesus illustrated with the story of the Good Samaritan, teaching that our neighbor is anyone in need. The Samaritan showed he was "good" because he had compassion—showed pity and concern—for the stranger who had been beaten. He did all he could to help him until the man could help himself. We are to do likewise in Jesus' name.

On the shore of the Sea of Galilee when the resurrected Jesus cooked breakfast for His disciples, He tested Peter's love for Him three times and then gave him the command "Feed my sheep." In other words, "Because you love me, Peter, stop living for yourself. Get busy teaching others the truth about me with love and devotion for me." In Peter's replies there seemed to be a growing attitude of humility. As far as we know he never went back to "fishing" for fish, but spent his time "fishing for men." This was far more satisfying and exciting and brought eternal results. This is our calling.

In what ways did Jesus set an example for all Christians in regard to others? As a boy He obeyed Joseph and Mary and was subject to their authority.

As a young man growing up in Nazareth, He "increased in wisdom and stature, and in favour with God and man" (Luke 2:52). Here was a teen-ager who pleased God, was popular, strong, and well behaved.

To His unbelieving and critical brothers, Jesus was polite and kind; for He knew they did not understand Him or His purpose for living (John 7:1-5). After His resurrection at least two of His brothers became believers and wrote the epistles of James and Jude.

To His disciples, His closest friends, Jesus taught about God and gave them God's truth (John 17:14, 17). He loved them (even Judas) unto the end (John 13:1). He prayed for unity among them (and all believers), so that the world might believe in Him (John 17:20, 21, 23). This great love of Jesus in the hearts of those eleven disciples (Judas was excluded) bound them closely together. How strange and varied were their backgrounds, their occupations, their personalities and dispositions; and yet He was able to make them one in Him, to be molded together by the power of His love.

> Blest be the tie that binds our hearts in Christian love,
> The fellowship of kindred minds is like to that above.

Christian fellowship and service can be likened to an old-fashioned wagon wheel with its hub, spokes, and rim. The hub in the center represents Christ. The spokes represent Christians connected to Christ. The nearer the spokes come to the hub, the nearer they come to one another. So it is in our Christian lives: the nearer we come to Christ, the nearer we are to one another in fellowship. Christ, the hub, is the center of importance in God's wheel.

The rim, which runs along on the road, can go in no given direction by itself. It must be attached to the hub by the spokes. The spokes are braces extending from the hub to the rim, but can go nowhere by themselves. Strong, well-made spokes attached to the hub and extending out to the rim make a wheel that can go safely down any road in any direction to fulfill the purpose for which it was made.

So it is with Christians: God wants us not only to be like spokes in a wheel attached to the hub, Jesus Christ, in close fellowship with Him and other Christians, but to extend our usefulness as strong, God-made servants to go to others in any direction He chooses.

54

Jesus covered very little territory in miles during His short ministry of three and one-half years, but He loved all ages and kinds of people. Wherever He went He showed His love in kindly actions.

Jesus called a little child to Him (Matthew 18:2), and the child felt comfortable and happy with Him. He valued one small child as being of importance, not to be despised, and later on He blessed a group of children (Matthew 19:13-15).

He healed Peter's mother-in-law, an older woman whom He thought worth helping in her need.

Mary, Martha, and Lazarus were the special friends whom He loved and with whom He often visited in their home at Bethany. To Martha, who had become jittery, worried, and bothered preparing an elaborate meal, Jesus gave a rebuke in a kind way by telling her that Mary had chosen wisely in spending her time listening to Him talk about eternal and spiritual matters. Mary had believed Him when He said He would soon die, for she anointed Him with her precious oil for His burial ahead of time. Her private talk with Jesus had opened her understanding of God's purpose for His Son.

Jesus wept with Mary and Martha after Lazarus' death because He was troubled and grieved. He sorrowed with Mary and Martha in their loss. He deeply felt their distress. He was a "man of sorrows and acquainted with grief."

From the agony of the cross, Jesus thought of His mother, Mary—of her suffering and her need above His own—by committing her to the care of the one most qualified to love and understand what she was going through, the beloved disciple, John (John 19:26, 27).

From the cross Jesus heard the cry of the dying thief asking to be remembered when He, the King of the Jews, would come into His kingdom and gave him the good news: "Today shalt thou be with me in paradise." Jesus in His suffering was still thinking of and responding to the need of others.

After His resurrection Jesus revealed Himself in special ways to Mary Magdalene, to Thomas with his doubts, to Peter in his distress for having denied his Lord, to James as well as to two believers walking on the road to Emmaus, to the eleven disciples gathered in an upper room, to a few on the shore of Galilee early one morning, and to over "five hundred brethren at once."

In this way they were all convinced that the crucified Jesus had been resurrected and was now alive forevermore—"declared to be the Son of God with power, according to the spirit of holiness, by the resurrection from the dead: By whom we have received grace and apostleship, for obedience to the faith among all nations, for his name" (Romans 1:4, 5). In other words the knowledge and power of Christ's resurrection must be shared by people in all nations through His witnesses—that is, through us.

> When Jesus has found you, tell others the story
> That my loving Savior is your Savior too:
> They pray that your Savior will bring them to glory
> And prayer will be answered—'twas answered for you.

If the gospel is to be made known to others, the place to begin is in the family circle (perhaps the hardest place of all).

The Bible makes it plain that the human family unit is important in God's sight. Husbands and wives, fathers and mothers, children, brothers and sisters, and servants are included in the picture (Ephesians 5:22-6:9).

Christians should marry Christians to establish a godly home. A mixed marriage is an unequal yoke that is displeasing to God.

Marriage is a picture of a believer's union with Christ and should not be broken. Jesus said a man and his wife are one flesh: "What therefore God hath joined together, let not man put asunder" (Matthew 19:6). The church is the body of Christ. Each believer is a member of the body, joined to it for eternity, and will not be cut off.

Many of us believe that marriage of divorced persons is unscriptural from such passages as Mark 10:11, 12; Romans 7: 2, 3; and I Corinthians 7:10, 11. These verses state plainly that it is not right to remarry and, in the first two verses, (Mark 10: 11, 12) that adultery is committed by one party or the other, regardless of the cause for divorce.

There are at least four definite reasons why I believe remarriage of divorced persons who are Christians is wrong:

1. The Scriptures forbid it.
2. The type of the believer's union with Christ is broken.

3. It is a very poor testimony, it lowers standards, and it hurts the cause of Christ.
4. Where there are children there is for them deep hurt and insecurity.

How are the members of a family to act toward one another as Christians?

A husband is to love his wife as himself. He is to cherish (hold dear and prize) her, value, care for, protect and treasure her all her days.

A wife is to submit to her husband, as head of the family; to be subject to him; to reverence or respect her husband (Ephesians 5:33). She need not fear to respond in these ways to a man who loves her as himself and is willing to die for her.

A father is to use controlled discipline over his children to win their respect and bring them up with Christian teaching (Ephesians 6:4). A father should be willing to listen to a child—"to communicate" with him—and should try to understand him and to win his confidence.

A mother should be as Timothy's mother: a woman with "unfeigned faith" in God—a woman who has a vital, living, real trust in the Lord and who prays for her family and gets her prayers answered according to the will of God. Hannah, Samuel's mother, is an example of this as she gave her little boy back to God.

Children are to be obedient to their fathers and mothers in the Lord (Ephesians 6:1-3) and to honor their parents that it may be well with them. This is right in God's sight and best for the children.

Christian parents are of great value to children; many of us older people look back with gratitude to God for having given us godly parents.

Brothers and sisters are to love one another—not as Cain, who hated Abel and killed him (I John 2:9-11; I John 3:11, 12), but as those who love God and love one another (I John 4:11, 20, 21).

A father and mother in the Kentucky Mountains raised a family of nine children. There was little money, there were few possessions, and there was hard work for every member of the family to do to take care of the daily chores and to raise enough food to meet daily needs.

57

The children were normal children—working together, playing together, fighting together, and defending one another when neighbor children tried to pick a fight with any one of them. There was always love for one another in this family; but when some of the members became true Christians, that love became intensified and expressed itself in many Christ-like ways. I know, because the oldest daughter has lived with me for over twenty-five years.

An uneducated mother of a large family in an isolated place with a problem husband, became a Christian. Her only hope was prayer to God to help her family to have an education, to be saved, and to have a chance to make good in life. This seemed impossible. The oldest son was able to get away from home to receive a doctor's education. He married a nurse, who cooperated with him in giving the other members of his family any education they would or could take. Those who responded to this opportunity turned out to be the answer to their mother's prayers by living useful, Christian lives. In turn they loved, appreciated, and respected her. Here were a praying mother and an unselfish brother and sisters who loved the members of their family. Those who became Christians have continued to show loving concern about the spiritual lives of their relatives.

Servants (helpers or employees) in the Christian home are to obey instructions from their employers in singleness of heart as unto Christ (Ephesians 6:5-7). They are to work hard as if they were working for the Lord Jesus.

Masters or employers are to be just and fair, not using threats, not showing partiality or favoritism, but being kind and considerate (Ephesians 6:9) as God is to them. There would be no need of labor unions if there was this attitude between employers and employees.

A home where Christian love operates, as God intends it to, is a stronghold of power in a community.

Then there are usually neighbors who are others to be considered and to act toward as Christians.

Jesus said that we should love our neighbors as ourselves. That means we will treat them as we would want them to treat us.

Paul in Romans 13:10 said, "Love worketh no ill to his neighbor." If we love our neighbors we will not want to harm them by immoral acts, murder, stealing, lying, and coveting what they have (Romans 13:9) but will love and help them in every possible way.

There is nothing nicer than to live in a community of good Christian neighbors who love one another.

> Look all around you, find someone in need,
>   Help somebody today!
> Though it be little—a neighborly deed—
>   Help somebody today!
>
> Many are wanting a kind, loving word,
>   Help somebody today!
> Thou hast a message, O let it be heard,
>   Help somebody today!
>
> Many have burdens too heavy to bear,
>   Help somebody today!
> Grief is the portion of some everywhere,
>   Help somebody today!
>
> Help somebody today, somebody along life's way;
> Let sorrow be ended, the friendless befriended,
>   Oh, help somebody today!

If we live for Christ in this world we will have enemies as He did. How are we to act toward them?

Jesus said in Matthew 5:44, "Love your enemies, bless them that curse you, do good to them that hate you, and pray for them which despitefully use you." He practiced what He preached. Judas was Jesus' enemy, yet Jesus prayed for him. When Judas betrayed Jesus with a kiss, the Lord called him "Friend." On the cross He cried, "Father, forgive them [His enemies] for they know not what they do."

To Pilate and Herod He was quiet and polite.

To His enemies the Pharisees and scribes He witnessed over and over again, very patiently, showing who He was. When they rejected His teachings, He denounced them as hypocrites and warned them of their doom: "Woe, woe unto you."

Jesus told His followers that if someone would hit them on one cheek they were to turn the other also. A young missionary friend

59

of mine in South America was stating her belief to a local Roman Catholic priest who did not agree with her. He became infuriated and gave her a hard smack on one cheek. She hesitated a moment and then quickly turned her other cheek toward him, literally obeying her Lord's command. Startled, the priest backed off and quickly walked away.

Jesus set us an example in His attitude toward all sorts of people. His motive was love for God and love for men.

He healed lepers; He cured the servant of a Roman centurion; He cast out demons; He healed the blind, the deaf, the lame; He fed the hungry multitudes and healed all who came to Him, expecting nothing in return.

Jesus was not partial. He was kind to a Greek woman to whom He did not come (she was not a Jewess), for He came unto the Jews. Jesus loved the rich young ruler who did not love Him. He was kind to the woman caught in adultery, did not condemn her, but told her not to sin again. Jesus spent time talking to Nicodemus, a Jewish ruler, about spiritual things. He offered the hated Samaritan woman "living water" through faith in Him.

Jesus did not live for Himself; He lived for God and others. So should every Christian. That is the joyous life. It has been said that the happiest people in the world are Christian missionaries. Why? Because they live for Christ and others, not for themselves.

Young people are needed today in America to lead out for Jesus Christ and not to go along with the crowd who are trying to wreck themselves and take others with them. Paul told Timothy, "Let no man despise thy youth; but be thou an example of the believers, in word, in conversation, in charity, in spirit, in faith, in purity" (I Timothy 4:12).

A young man, twenty-three years of age, was killed in a boat accident on a lake in Kentucky. It was a tragedy to all of us who knew him, for he had lived a quiet, useful, unselfish life. He was considered a Christian because he had joined the church as a young boy (I was present at that service and thought, "He knows what he is doing.") He attended Sunday school regularly, went to church when he became older, and when asked, took part in the services. After church he talked to people and was friendly with the older ones as well at those near his age. They all loved him, for he loved others.

60

When this young man went to college things often got hard. He asked the Lord to help him and received the answer, for he believed in prayer.

He was good to his mother and father and considerate of his grandmother, with whom he spent a great deal of time talking about conditions and ways of helping people. She said, "He never made a big show of anything. It was just a wonderful love he felt for people and the Lord; it seems as though he could never do enough to help anyone."

He visited the sick, helped the poor and needy, and tried to convince his students in school and other places that drugs would ruin their lives. In one case he saw a young boy whom he knew sitting alone beside the highway as he drove along. He turned the car around, drove back, stopped, and asked the boy whether he was all right. The boy had some dope and was getting ready to take it. The young school teacher spent an hour talking to him and finally persuaded the boy to throw the dope away, go on to school and prepare to live a clean, useful life. The boy did what he suggested.

As a school teacher, a coach (he loved sports), as a member of the rescue squad, and with the boys in his Little League Softball Team, he tried to influence all with whom he worked to live clean lives and make them count for the Lord and others.

He wanted the love and respect of those he worked with more than anything else. At his funeral and in the days following, his friends showed that love and respect for him in every possible way. He had lived not for self but for others.

> Lord help me live from day to day
> In such a self-forgetful way
> That even when I kneel to pray,
> My prayer shall be for—OTHERS.
>
> Help me in all the work I do
> To ever be sincere and true
> And know that all I'd do for you,
> Must needs be done for—OTHERS.
>
> Others, Lord, yes, others,
> Let this my motto be.
> Help me to live for others,
> That I might live like Thee.

Christian Behavior Toward Others

1. Speak wisely to unbelievers. I Peter 3:15
2. Be concerned, compassionate, courteous. Matthew 9:36; I Peter 3:8
3. Be kind, tenderhearted, forgiving. Ephesians 4:32
4. Be unselfish and humble. Philippians 2:3, 4
5. Do good to all, especially to Christians, widows and orphans. Galatians 6:10; James 1:27
6. Show feelings of mercy and true love. Romans 12:9, 10
7. Be hospitable. Hebrews 13:2; I Peter 4:9
8. Speak not evil but good words (Ephesians 4:29); not using flattery, for, as has been said: "Flattery is one man's meanness taking advantage of another man's weakness."
9. Speak the truth, not lies. Ephesians 4:25
10. Do not hit back; be honest. Romans 12:17
11. Comfort and edify (instruct for spiritual growth). I Thessalonians 5:11
12. Share in others' joys and sorrows; be interested; be a good listener. Romans 12:15
13. Please one's neighbour. Romans 15:2
14. Cheer and encourage. Acts 27:22, 25.
15. Strengthen weak Christians. Luke 22:32
16. Restore a backslider. Galatians 6:1
17. Refresh Christian friends. II Timothy 1:16
18. Choose right kind of companions. II Thessalonians 3:6, 11; II Corinthians 6:14
19. Do not be a stumbling block. Romans 14:13
20. Do not go to law with other Christians. I Corinthians 6:1
21. Do not forget those who taught us God's Word. Hebrews 13:7
22. Live peaceably with all men. Romans 12:18
23. Do not stay angry with one another. Ephesians 4:26

A close relative of mine made it a rule of his life never to go to sleep at night if he was angry with his wife, but always to settle any quarrel with love and prayer. This rule has made a happy marriage for nearly forty years.

24. Do not be critical. Matthew 7:1

Many years ago I traveled to the Far East with a relative of my father. She continually criticized other travelers for their selfishness, greediness at the table, and wanting the best of everything for themselves. It was not long before I noticed that the very things she criticized in others were her own outstanding faults, a fact revealed in Romans 2:1: "Thou that judgest doest the same things." People shunned her and I was embarrassed to be her traveling companion. I learned a lesson then I hope I shall never forget: selfishness and criticism are most unattractive and are sins to be conquered.

25. Confess your faults one to another, and pray for one another.
    James 5:16

We should not do as two Christian women I knew who decided they were good enough friends to have a "truth party" to tell each other their faults. The "party" did not last long, for the first one to speak so infuriated the other one she walked away and would not speak to her "friend" for a year. They neglected "to pray for one another" as James said.

26. By love serve one another. Galatians 5:13

A little nine-year-old girl named Rita was walking with a missionary at an outing in the woods near Innsbruck, Austria. As the missionary began singing quietly, "Whosoever will to the Lord may come," Rita interrupted with the words "He's inside already."

With surprise the missionary asked what she meant.

Rita replied, "I don't remember the day He came in, but I know He is in."

"How do you know?" questioned the missionary.

"He has forgiven all my sins and has changed my life completely," she said.

Then she explained how she, Rita, and her older sister never got along. Once, after an argument, she had been given the first choice of selecting her dessert from a dish of strawberries. She picked out all the nice ones for herself and left the bad ones for her unsaved sister. The Holy Spirit convicted her about this. She said to herself, "Stop. This doesn't please the Lord." Instead of going to the table to selfishly devour the best berries, she took the dish of good berries to her sister and contentedly ate the bad ones herself.

27. Above all things, pray:
> For all men to be saved. I Timothy 2:1, 4
> For all in authority for peace in the nations. I Timothy 2:2
> For all saints (saved people). Ephesians 6:18 For an individual. Romans 15:30, 31
> For one another. Colossians 1:3, 4:12
> Giving thanks for all things. Ephesians 5:20

April 17, 1970, was a date long to be remembered. Three astronauts were returning from near the moon in a crippled space craft, the *Apollo 13*.

The people of the world and especially the people in the United States watched their television sets with hopes mingled with fears and ardent prayers for a safe return.

What a thrill and what a relief it was to see that capsule coming down through the clouds with parachutes fully open! Prayers of thanksgiving went up as the men put their feet down on the deck of the aircraft carrier *Iwo Jima.*

Beside our TV set we joined in prayer with the chaplain as he thanked God for His grace and the magnificent job that was done by the experts at headquarters in Houston, Texas, and the three men in the capsule. The authorities in Houston gave instructions from their book. The men coming through space followed the instructions given to them from a copy of the same book and made a perfect landing. (Let us not forget that we have a book, The Bible, to guide us to a perfect landing.)

What an illustration this is of "fervent prayer" and what God can do when Christians cooperate with Him in doing His work—bringing His lost creation back home to Him—in His way, according to His commands!

It is great to be in touch with the Commander-in-Chief in heaven, to get our instructions from Him through His book, and to obey them in the power of the Holy Spirit.

After I graduated from boarding school many years ago, a classmate and I volunteered to help as counselors at a girls' summer camp in New England. I am sure we were not qualified for the job nor successful in doing it, for we were not asked to return the next summer.

Those weeks were not wasted for me because of something I heard and never forgot. It was an explanation of the verses in II Timothy 2:19-21 that touched me and even made me weep. Our Bible teacher, a lovely Christian lady, pointed out in verse 19 that "the Lord knoweth them that are his. And, Let everyone that nameth the name of Christ depart from iniquity." As she went on into verse 20 she mentioned the vessels of gold and of silver, wood and earth that were in a great house. Each vessel (probably a serving dish or pitcher) was different in appearance and costliness. The importance of the vessel was not in its beauty or monetary value but in its usefulness to the master of the house. In order to be used it must be cleansed to be made "meet" (fit) for his service (verse 21) and prepared unto every good work. Imagine a wealthy "master" pouring pure water from a filthy silver pitcher to refresh his guests!

Then Miss P. said that Christians were the "vessels" (containers) needing to be cleansed and filled for God's service. I stayed to talk to her after the class to tell her I wanted to be a vessel God could use and asked her to pray for me. She did so and then told me that it is the dipping out, overflowing, or pouring out of the contents of the vessel that brings refreshing and strength to others. If I would ask God to cleanse me, fill me, and overflow through me, He would do it; for "we have this treasure [the light of the knowledge of the glory of God in the face of Jesus Christ] in earthen vessels, that the excellency of the power may be of God, and not of us" (II Corinthians 4:6, 7).

> Is your life a channel of blessing?
> Is the love of God flowing thro' you?
> Are you telling the lost of the Savior?
> Are you ready His service to do?
>
> We cannot be channels of blessing
> If our lives are not free from all sin;
> We will barriers be and a hindrance
> To those we are trying to win.

CHORUS

Make me a channel of blessing today,
Make me a channel of blessing I pray;
My life possessing, my service blessing,
Make me a channel of blessing today.

* * * * *

Channels only, blessed Master,
But with all Thy wondrous power
Flowing through us, Thou canst use us
Ev'ry day and ev'ry hour.

CHAPTER FIVE

Toward

Things—God's Provision

While we look not at the things which are seen, but at the things which are not seen: for the things which are seen are temporal; but the things which are not seen are eternal" (II Corinthians 4:18).

Here we have a verse of Scripture which contrasts temporal things with eternal things—things of time and things of eternity.

In Romans 15:27 we have the mention of carnal (worldly) things with spiritual things. Carnal things, temporal things: What are they? We see them and live with them all the time, and they are necessary in our lives. In this modern world "things" seem to be essential.

To exist we must have food and water. To be comfortable and decent, we must have clothing. Houses with furniture and furnishings, jobs, education, travel, the family car or cars, newspapers, magazines, books, telephones, radio and television—all seem important in the life of the average American family.

Churches with beautiful air-conditioned sanctuaries, lovely organs, pianos, hymn books, flowers, and comfortable pews abound in our land. Expensive additions for Sunday school and religious educational purposes are available for training children and young people "religiously." Sad to say, these buildings are not always used to produce spiritual results and to prepare people for eternity, because Jesus Christ is not preached or taught to those who attend. They see and hear the things that are around them, but not the Lord Jesus Christ, who died for them.

Jesus knew how important "things" were to the people of His day when He talked to His disciples in Matthew 6:25-34. He warned His followers not to concentrate on, or worry about, food, drink, or clothing, as the Gentiles (heathen, unbelievers) spent their time doing, but to trust their heavenly Father, who knew their needs, to provide for them. Their lives were more important than things. "Is not the life more than meat [food], and the body than raiment [clothing]?" (verse 25b).

They were to seek first the kingdom of God and His righteousness and all these "things" would be added unto them. They would find that God would gladly give them the things they needed (and more too, sometimes) if they gave Him the first place in their lives.

This is good counsel for us today, when the emphasis is often on things and people are scrambling to have all they can get by hook or crook. They think they are valued by what they have, whereas the important thing is what they are.

Because things occupy so much of our time and thinking, we as Christians must guard against their taking first place in our lives.

Satan tempted Christ in the matter of hunger when he told Him to command the stones to be made bread (Matthew 4:3). In His answer Jesus, in verse 4, put the emphasis in the right place: "It is written, Man shall not live by bread alone, but by every word that proceedeth out of the mouth of God."

Again, the devil took Him up on a high mountain (verse 8) and showed Him all the kingdoms of the world and the glory of them and said, "All these things [power, prestige, ownership] will I give thee, if thou wilt fall down and worship me." The Lord Jesus put first things first, in right relationship when, quoting from Deuteronomy 6:13, He told the devil, "Thou shalt worship the Lord thy God, and him only shalt thou serve."

Jesus Christ was interested first and only in doing God's will and not allowing any thing to interfere with that.

Eternal things were most important to Jesus. Prayer and fellowship with His Father, preaching to the lost, doing miracles to reveal God's power, and obeying His Father's commands were the things He loved and did.

Yet the Lord Jesus Christ, while here on earth, needed and used temporal or carnal things.

He used a mountain as a place of prayer before choosing His disciples (Luke 6:12, 13); as a place to teach His disciples (Matthew 5:1, 2); as a place to heal the multitudes

(Matthew 15:29-31); as a place to pray before walking on the sea (Matthew 14:23-32); as a place to feed the five thousand (John 6:3-14); as a place for His transfiguration (Luke 9:28-31); as a place for escape from those who wanted to make Him a king (John 6:15); and as a place from which to ascend home to heaven (Acts 1:9, 12).

Jesus used a ship in which to rest in sleep and from which to calm the tempest (Matthew 8:23-27); for travel (Matthew 9:1), and as a pulpit from which to teach a great multitude of people by the seaside (Luke 5:3).

Jesus used Peter's home to heal Peter's mother-in-law from her high fever and later at the door of the house to heal many sick people and cast out many devils (Mark 1:29-34).

He used the occasion of a wedding to perform His first miracle of turning water into wine (John 2:1-11).

He used a well (Jacob's) to talk to a sinful Samaritan woman (John 4:6, 7, 29, 39) and cause her and many of her neighbors to believe in Him as the Christ, the expected Messiah.

He used a seaside (a beach) from which to preach (Mark 2:13).

He used a synagogue in Capernaum to teach true doctrine with authority because He knew what He was talking about and practiced what He taught (Mark 1:21, 22). While in the synagogue He freed a man from an unclean spirit (verses 23-27) and revealed God's power in and through Him.

He used the temple to talk to the chief priests, scribes, and elders (Mark 11:27, 28) and to show the true purpose of the temple for prayer and worship by driving out the money changers.

He used the loaves and fishes of a small boy to feed the five thousand and thereby to show compassion and to reveal His power (John 6:9, 11, 14). The next day He pointed the same people to Himself as the "living bread" who could feed them spiritually (John 6:27, 35, 57).

He used the sabbath day for teaching a lesson on food for the hungry and God's purpose for that day of rest: "The sabbath was made for man" (Mark 2:27). In chapter 3:1-5 His healing the man with the withered hand in the synagogue showed it was lawful to do good on the sabbath day, to bring benefit and kindness to needy people.

He used a fig tree as an example of faith and prayer (Mark 11:13-24).

He used money from a fish's mouth to pay His and Peter's tribute tax and to show He was an obedient Jew (Matthew 17: 24, 27).

He used Lazarus' grave to prove His resurrection power (John 11:25, 41-44).

He used a towel, a basin, and water for washing the disciples' feet in order to teach them a lesson on humility (John 13:4, 5) and the need for cleansing from daily contact with the world.

He used an unbroken colt for His triumphant entry into Jerusalem (Luke 19:30-35).

He used a guest chamber of a friend to hold the Passover feast with His disciples (Mark 14:12-16).

He used a garden, Gethsemane, as a place for prayer and soul struggle in facing the agony of the cross (Mark 14:32-34).

He used a cross on Calvary's hill on which to die for sinners (Luke 23:33).

He used another man's tomb to be buried in and from which to rise again on the third day triumphant over death (Luke 23:50, 52, 53; Luke 24:1-6).

He used coals for a fire to cook a breakfast of fish and bread for His disciples after the resurrection and served Peter and those with him in order to show He was alive and that He cared for them (John 21:9, 10, 13).

If we carefully read the four Gospels, we will see that everything Jesus used was not for selfish purposes nor for self-gratification, but to please and glorify God and to accomplish His Father's will and purpose while here on earth.

Jesus had nothing of His own—no place to lay His head, but everything He needed was provided just when He needed it because He obeyed His Father in heaven. "All these things" were "added" unto Him, for He sought "first the kingdom of God and His righteousness."

Things were given to Jesus by His friends. Mary gave her very precious ointment from her alabaster box, pouring it on His head because she believed His word that He would soon be crucified. It was probably her most valuable possession, which she poured out in faith and love, believing Him to be her Messiah.

There were those who entertained Jesus in their homes as He traveled about: Peter, Mary, Martha, and Lazarus; Matthew, Zacchaeus, and Simon the leper.

The lad gave Him the loaves and fishes; the man lent Him his unbroken colt; a friend lent Him the guest chamber; the Roman government provided the cross; Joseph of Arimathea gave Him his own tomb, and Nicodemus brought spices to put on the clean cloth Joseph of Arimathea used to wrap around His body. These gifts were given to meet His need or to show respect and love for Him.

How do we use things these days? Do we use a mountain, a ship (or boat), a home, a wedding, a beach, a lake or ocean, a place of worship, food, the Lord's day, a horse or pony, a guest room, a garden, a tree, a breakfast on the beach or a grave in a cemetery (to continually weep and mourn) for selfish purposes?

If we follow Jesus' example we will not.

Mountain climbing, boating, horseback riding, swimming, and fishing are all good sports and are usually just for fun or exercise.

Houses, weddings, food, picnics, guest rooms, gardens, and trees are used for daily living, beauty, and entertainment.

The Lord's day and a place of worship are often neglected or used to suit a person's whim.

Jesus set us an example about all of these things. They are to be used for God's glory and not for selfish purposes. His heavenly Father had provided them for Him, and He never failed to use them according to God's will.

Jesus was the Creator, the "Word of God." "All things were made by Him" (John 1:1, 3). He knew the purpose for which mankind was created. God gave Him (and us) intelligence and physical strength to use the things He created for man's own good and for fellowship with the Father.

Jesus knew the danger of human beings putting things or possessions first when He warned the disciples to beware of covetousness and said that "a man's life consisteth not in the abundance of the things which he possesseth" (Luke 12:15).

Then He gave them an illustration of a rich farmer who kept the fruit and produce he had raised from his good land for himself so he could take his ease, eat, drink, and be merry. But that very night God required his soul and called him a fool, for who would get all the things the man had worked hard to provide for Himself? He could not take them with him.

Things today are food, drink, clothing, personal possessions, time, days, jobs, homes, lands, hours, words, books, playthings,

71

sports, musical instruments, cars, planes, bicycles, motorcycles, television, and whatever we have to use.

Have you who are reading this chapter ever thought about the things you like best? That might be interesting. I asked a class of teen-agers to tell me what things they loved best. What did they enjoy most? The answers were sports, music, books, TV, and swimming. As I was reading this chapter to check and improve it, I suddenly thought, "What do I like best?" Then ideas came popping into my head. A good dependable car was first; then other ideas followed rapidly: nice clothes, good food, good books, good music, lovely flowers, pretty birds, nice pets, a comfortable and pretty home, and, best of all, challenging Christian service.

Then I asked myself, "Why do I like these things?" Well, I need a car for transportation, clothes for a proper appearance, food for health and strength, books for instruction and entertainment, music for relaxation and pleasure, flowers, birds and pets for interest, a home for comfort and enjoyment, and Christian service for complete satisfaction.

These things are all God's loving provision to meet my needs as a child of His, in order to enable me to serve and glorify Him in my sphere of life.

"Things" are for now; they are temporal, not eternal.

"Things" are carnal—of this world, not spiritual.

Esau was a man who was "profane" or carnal. He loved food more than a spiritual blessing; so he sold his birthright to Jacob, his brother, for a mess of pottage. In contrast Jacob, though tricky, had a desire for spiritual and eternal matters and received the blessing.

In the New Testament we have the contrast of Paul and Demas. Paul said: " . . . what things were gain to me, those I counted loss for Christ. . . . I count all things but loss . . . I have suffered the loss of all things . . . that I may win Christ" (Philippians 3:7, 8).

Demas was one who minded "earthly things" (Philippians 3: 19), for in II Timothy 4:10, Paul wrote, "Demas hath forsaken me, having loved this present world."

No wonder John, in his old age, needed to write the commandment: "Love not the world, neither the things that are in the world. If any man love the world, the love of the Father is not in him." These are serious words by which we should check our motives and actions regarding "things."

In 1 Corinthians 10:5, 6, Paul wrote about the behavior of the people of Israel as Moses led them through the wilderness: "With many of them God was not well pleased." They lusted or desired "evil things" and were examples to us that we should not do likewise. They gave their gold jewelry to Aaron to make a golden calf. Then they ate, drank, danced, and worshiped the idol, contrary to God's Law. This was carnality at its worst.

In the matter of food, drink, and clothes for the days in which we live we Christians must know the teaching of the New Testament regarding these important everyday things.

Food is a must if we are to be strengthened to do God's work. It is plentiful, but expensive, and is bought and sold in abundance and is often wasted. Moderation, a proper diet, and a good conscience should be a guide to us in this matter.

Daniel was an example of a young man who used simple, nourishing food to make him healthy and strong.

Much time is spent about food: producing, securing, preparing, and consuming it. It seems that a great deal of, perhaps too much, conversation revolves around food—conversation that should edify others.

An amusing anecdote appeared recently in a local newspaper. A lady wanted to make a hurried telephone call on a party line. When she picked up the receiver she heard one woman talking to another about cooking beans; so she hung up and waited a few minutes. Later, when she went back to the phone and picked up the receiver, the women were still talking about the beans; so she said, "Lady, I smell your beans burning." The woman gave a yell and hung up the receiver.

Drink is necessary for our bodily needs and pure water is the most healthful drink of all. Look around and see the kind of drinks people are substituting for water. They are too numerous to name. Too much time is taken even by Christian "socializing" around some form of drink: coffee, tea, soft drinks. There is nothing wrong with them in themselves, but in the many minutes often spent in selfish, unnecessary conversation rather than in "redeeming the time" with stimulating, helpful words about the Lord Jesus and His cause. From Paul in Romans 14:17 we have the right answer to this matter of eating and drinking: " . . . the kingdom of God is not meat and drink; but righteousness and peace, and joy in the holy Ghost [Spirit]."

The emphasis for the Christian should always be on "eternal things" even as we use the "temporal things" we need. Our conversation while eating and drinking can be glorifying to God as we talk of His Son.

In the second chapter of Acts, verses 46 and 47, we read that believers "breaking bread from house to house, did eat their meat with gladness and singleness of heart, praising God." The result was strengthening fellowship, not self-indulgence or wasted time, which weaken.

We need to ask God for guidance in these matters as in the following hymn:

Guide me, O Thou great Jehovah,
Pilgrim through this barren land;
I am weak but Thou art mighty,
Hold me with Thy powerful hand.

Bread of heaven, feed me till I want no more.
Bread of heaven, feed me till I want no more.

Open now the crystal fountain,
Whence the healing waters flow;
Let the fiery, cloudy pillar
Lead me all my journey through.

Strong Deliverer, Be Thou still my strength and shield.
Strong Deliverer, Be Thou still my strength and shield.

Clothing occupies an important place in our daily lives. What about today with extreme and changing fashions for women and men? How should Christians dress to attract others to Jesus Christ?

"Man looketh on the outward appearance, but God looketh on the heart" (I Samuel 16:7). If our hearts are right with God, our outward appearance should reveal that fact.

Have you ever asked yourself, "How would I feel if I wore these clothes and met the best Christian I know?" That person would be a representative of Christ as well as I. If my appearance shocked him and embarrassed me, I would be dishonoring my Lord.

In I Timothy 2:9 women are instructed to dress moderately, suitably, not elaborately. Christian women should be noticed for their kindness and good character, not for their adornments.

In Proverbs 31:22 the virtuous woman's "clothing is silk and purple." In verse 25 "strength and honor are her clothing." We see that she dresses beautifully and her clothing forms a picture frame for her excellent character. This should be a guide to us today.

We should not let the power of wearing apparel, jewelry, and make-up grip us. The outward adorning should be such that the "meek and quiet spirit," which is in every Christian woman by the indwelling Holy Spirit and "which is in the sight of God of great price," can be readily seen (I Peter 3:4).

These present days of "mini-skirts," which are hopefully supposed to be going out of style, are a challenge for a Christian woman to dress suitably.

Muslim students from Africa who have come to America or England for further education have been shocked and offended by the indecent dress of Christian women, especially students.

One student said, "Why is your country so full of immorality? Islam is far better, for we have no drinking and we do not permit the open nakedness of women as you do. I am a much stronger Muslim now that I have seen what little good Christianity does."

Another student wrote a letter saying, "It was my observation that the girls were not fair to the fellows. The very short dresses are not appropriate, particularly in a church school. In a land in which people show no concern about the kind of living that accompanies improper exposure of the body, I would expect that Christian young people would take advantage of this opportunity to bear witness to Jesus Christ."

"There in your land," wrote another student, "most people don't believe in God. They are clever and rich—what difference does God make? I think my people, too, will give up their belief in God and will worship the God of things as you do."

What about men's appearance? Surely a Christian man should dress conservatively and becomingly in keeping with the present styles. He should be neat, clean, and as attractive as possible for the task in which he is engaged. Every sort of clothing is available at varying prices from which the Christian man can choose for the occupation or profession he is following.

The Lord Jesus was criticized for everything He said or did, but as far as I can read He was never criticized for his attire. He grew "in favor with God and man," and at the time of His arrest and trial not one thing could be found wrong with Him. His outer garments were good enough for the soldiers to gamble over.

Each Christian should dress to look right, to be free from self-consciousness in order to be an effective witness for Jesus Christ in the place where God has put Him. Let us "adorn the doctrine of God, our Saviour, in all things," (Titus 2:10b) including clothing.

It is a good thing to pray about our clothes whether we shop and pay for them ourselves or whether we trust the Lord to give them to us in some other way.

It is exciting to pray before starting out on a shopping trip and to find the exact thing we need in a store without becoming exhausted and discouraged and possibly buying the wrong thing. (I have experienced this many times.)

The Lord Jesus said that God knew what we needed and that we should ask, and it would be given us (Matthew 7:7).

Homes and lands are very important in the life of every Christian. We must have a place to live in. A comfortable, attractive home is an asset if God provides for it in His own way and time.

A motto in our summer home (a double mobile home in the Kentucky Mountains) reads:

> Christ is the Head of this house,
> The unseen Host at every meal,
> The silent Listener to every conversation.

When we remember that motto, recognizing that the Lord Jesus is indeed the Head, the Host, the Listener, our home is a happy one and a place where true Christian fellowship is a delight.

The disciples were asked to leave homes, jobs, possessions, as Jesus had done, in order to do God's work.

Peter asked what the disciples would receive (what they would get out of following Jesus) because they had left all to follow Him (Matthew 19:27, 29). The Lord Jesus answered, "Everyone that hath forsaken houses . . . or lands for my name's sake, shall receive an hundredfold [one hundred times more]."

76

Those disciples could look forward to the "eternal things," which are not seen, to the things which are not carnal, but spiritual.

In the Old Testament we have the story of Abraham and Lot. Abraham gave Lot the first choice. Lot took the easy way of living in a house in the luxury and wickedness of Sodom and lost everything. Abraham stayed in tents in the mountains, worshiping God, and gained everything. Lot was carnal; Abraham was spiritual. Lot lived for time; Abraham lived for eternity: "For he looked for a city which hath foundations, whose builder and maker is God" (Hebrews 11:10).

Books are important things to many of us today. All sorts are available at popular prices. We should be very careful to select only books that are worth reading. The Bible is still the best seller and should be first on our list and in our homes.

The right reading is essential in a Christian's life. Books that inspire, edify, inform, and enlighten us are what we should read. Missionary biographies and Christian magazines enlarge our horizons and cause us to pray for missionaries.

In II Timothy 4:13 Paul asked that his cloke, his books, and especially his parchments (notebook and manuscripts) be brought to him. He needed his cloke for warmth and his books for the continuation of his important writing.

We are often thrilled by seeing some countries pictured graphically and beautifully in magazines. We know this world is filled with magnificent scenery, churches, buildings, and interesting historic places. Traveling with the right motive to see what God has made, or permitted man to erect, "enlarges our coast" and helps us understand His handiwork better.

A good way to spend a vacation is to visit different churches where the gospel is preached and to see missions, national and foreign, where the Lord Jesus is honored and the Holy Spirit is working.

Such things draw us close to Him and cause us to join with the hymn writer in the following verse often sung in churches:

> For the beauty of the earth,
> For the glory of the skies,
> For the love which from our birth
> Over and around us lies.

For the wonder of each hour
Of the day and of the night,
Hill and vale, and tree, and flower,
Sun and moon, and stars of light.

For Thy church that evermore
Lifts its holy hands above,
Offering up on every shore
Her pure sacrifice of love.

Christ, our God, to Thee we raise
This our hymn of grateful praise.

Business, jobs, writing, commerce, profession, housework, a
pastorate, church work, missionary work, or whatever a Christian
is responsible for are all things that are part of our daily lives.

Although Paul was a traveling missionary, he used his craft
(tentmaking) for a year and a half as he lived and preached in
Corinth. Paul was not lazy, nor did he impose on his friends, but
worked with his hands to meet his needs (Acts 20:34). Paul set the
example of obeying his own commands in II Thessalonians 3:8-10:
" . . . if any would not work, neither should he eat." He heard that
some at Thessalonica were "disorderly, working not at all,
but . . . busybodies" (verse 11). He commanded them to work,
and eat their own bread.

Idleness in Christians is dangerous to spiritual life.

Work, for the night is coming, work through the morning hours;
Work while the dew is sparkling; work 'mid springing flowers.
Work when the day grows brighter, work in the glowing sun;
Work, for the night is coming, when man's work is done.

Work, for the night is coming, work through the sunny noon;
Fill brightest hours with labor, rest comes sure and soon.
Give every flying minute something to keep in store;
Work, for the night is coming, when man works no more.

In the light of all this we have written, what are we to do in the
world of things? How are we to act toward them?

78

Paul says in I Corinthians 10:23, "All things are lawful [or allowed] for me, but all things are not expedient [or helpful]; all things are lawful for me, but all things edify not [are not good or constructive]."

As Christians we should set an example not to do anything that would cause another Christian to stumble or to be offended or made weak (Romans 14:21). Many weak, new babes in Christ have been harmed because a Christian, to whom they looked for an example to follow, has been un-Christlike in his attitude toward things.

Some friends of mine with three children all under six were visiting in a city where they had some close friends. The friends invited them all to have lunch in a good restaurant after church. At the close of the meal before leaving the table, the hostess put the embroidered cloth napkin she had used into her purse because she said it was unmarked.

The children looked amazed but said nothing until they got to the hotel room. The door was hardly closed until all wanted to know whether "auntie" paid for that napkin. When the parents said, "No, she didn't," they asked whether she stole it. Of course, to be truthful, the Christian parents had to say "Yes."

Love of the world, love of things has hindered many a child of God from being a true testimony for Jesus Christ.

Jesus told believers in I John 5:21, "Little children, keep yourselves from idols." We know that any "thing" we love before God is an idol.

> Jesus calls us from the worship
> Of the vain world's golden store,
> From each idol that would keep us,
> Saying, "Christian, love Me more."

The world and "the things of the world" belong to Satan. We learned earlier in this chapter that the devil offered them all to Jesus if He would worship him, Satan. Jesus refused them because it was not God's will nor time for Him to have them.

Satan is using the things of this world for his own purpose—to cheat God.

We know of churches that were once alive spiritually with gospel preaching, prayer, spiritual activity, and fellowship among members that have lost their vision and have become places where ministers now preach atheism.

We know of great universities that were started by godly men in order to provide Christian education with the Bible as the main textbook, but have departed from the Christian faith and now teach Communism.

We know of powerful businesses and corporations that were started by Christian men for God's glory and for a means of livelihood for the employees, but are now in the hands of those who no longer are Christian in principle or practice.

Such is also true of many hospitals and publishing houses. They were started to give spiritual as well as medical help to the sick and to furnish good Christian reading to the public. Now it seems as if many of them are out of the control of God and are under the control of Satan.

Satan is "the prince of this world" (John 12:31; John 14:30; John 16:11). "The whole world lieth in wickedness [the evil one]" (I John 5:19). But Jesus judged the world and all of its things on the cross and made it possible for every Christian to be delivered from their power.

We can, by faith, transfer the world and its things from Satan's account book to God's account book. When material things are under the Holy Spirit's control, they accomplish their proper purpose. Musical instruments especially can assist in worship and bless the hearts of those who are present, but I have seen musical instruments mean too much to Christians, thereby hindering a blessing.

We can check ourselves by asking: How is this thing affecting my relationship with my heavenly Father? Is it of this world or is it of God? Do I need it? Can He use it in my hands? Is it going to be in His way? Will my having it be a stumbling block to others? Does this church help or hurt my spiritual life? Can I be a true Christian while attending this college or university? Can I be a Spirit-filled Christian and continue working in this company or in this hospital or in this publishing house?

Let us as Christians use all these worldly things and places for God. We need the world and the world needs us; but we should not want or desire it or be weighed down by worldly things. We need to avoid their power over us. Instead we should hold them for God and not accumulate them for ourselves.

If God is in the center of our lives, we will keep no "thing" because we love it, but will be willing to let it go with no regrets when the time comes to do without it. I have a friend who loved golf, but when he became active and busy for the Lord there was no time for golf; so he gladly gave it up.

God has promised to supply all our needs "according to his riches in glory by Christ Jesus" (Philippians 4:19). He has also told us that with Christ he also gives us freely "all things" (Romans 8:32). That does not mean, of course, anything that would not be good for us.

We are to be content with such things as we have (Hebrews 13:5); for "godliness with contentment is great gain" (I Timothy 6:6), and "God . . . giveth us richly all things to enjoy" (I Timothy 6:17). . .

Therefore we are to act toward things as God's provision for us. We are to be thankful for them and use them as He purposes and to enjoy them with Him.

In these days when sports are very popular, a Christian who likes any sort of sport can use it to be a witness for Christ by being honest, clean in life and word, fair and disciplined to play a good game.

We must use things, whether great or small, as Jesus did—for our needs, for sharing with others, and for the glory of God. Then there is satisfaction, freedom, and no feeling of guilt.

> All for Jesus, all for Jesus!
> All my being's ransomed pow'rs:
> All my thoughts and words and doings,
> All my days and all my hours.

It is a good practice to dedicate to God anything important we buy or are given, whether it be a house, a car, a business, an education, a musical instrument, a journey, or a day.

Time is an important factor in our lives. Van Cliburn, the brilliant young pianist, met his pastor on the street in New York City one day. When asked what he had been doing, he told his minister that he had just finished a series of several concerts in succession. The minister marveled at the way the young man was able to carry such a heavy schedule of practice and performance. Van Cliburn gave a very telling answer when he said he had learned the secret of "the economy of effort."

Things never satisfy; Jesus does. Let us "turn . . . [our] eyes upon Jesus, look full in His wonderful face, and the things of earth will grow strangely dim, in the light of His glory and grace."

I should like to close this chapter with a personal testimony of God's dealing with me about things.

In boarding school in New York State, years ago, we were taught a little verse that I liked and that I wanted to have come true in my life:

> Lord Jesus, make Thyself to me,
> A living, bright reality;
> More present to Faith's vision keen
> Than any EARTHLY OBJECT seen;
> More dear, more intimately nigh
> Than even any earthly tie.

Some years went by filled with travel, gaiety, pretty clothes, an expensive car, and much dancing, which I loved because I loved music and rhythm. I suppose I put dancing first in my interests.

Then one summer at a Bible conference I became convicted of my selfish life and love of the things of this world and had a miserable time fighting the Holy Spirit.

A hymn my father often sang kept coming to me, and I would immediately put it out of my mind; but the next morning I would wake up with the words running through my thoughts. This continued for a week. Finally, I told the Lord I had given the world a try and had found that it and the things in it did not satisfy me. Therefore I would give Him a chance to see whether He would satisfy my longing heart. That was nearly fifty years ago, and the desire to go back to the old life has never returned. This is a part of the hymn the Lord used to bring me to Himself in complete deliverance from loving the world and its things:

> Nothing satisfies but Jesus,
> Bread of life to mortals given:
> May His presence now refresh us
> Like the morning dew from heaven.
>
> Since I heard the voice of Jesus,
> Since mine eyes beheld the King,

All my love, my heart's affection,
All I have, to Him I bring.

Chorus

Give me Jesus, give me Jesus,
Take the world, but give me Jesus;
To satisfy with every blessing,
His love and peace my soul possessing;
To all beside, my heart replies
There's naught but Jesus satisfies!

CHAPTER SIX

Toward

Money—God's Blessing or a Curse

What is this thing called "money"?

It can be cash, gold and silver bars, stocks, bonds, insurance, government bills, savings accounts, travelers' checks, credit cards, trust funds, scrip, stamps, or money in a checking account at a bank.

Money is called "wealth," "riches," or "means" and is possessed by those who either use it or keep it.

Coins, greenbacks (paper money), or checks mean nothing unless they are represented by silver bullion in the United States Treasury. One dollar equals that much silver; so it is true of a $10 bill; a $20, a $100, or a $1,000 bill.

Money is a medium of exchange. We are told that every dollar bill in circulation is spent once every twenty days. Money is important.

A child can spend seven cents for a candy bar, fifteen or twenty cents for a coke or pop, or swap a comic book for marbles. Anyone who sells a coke or candy bar cannot get it back if it has been drunk or eaten, nor can the seller eat the money he received. There has been a trade! The money is now his but of little value in itself, except to use as he desires. Money is anything which men agree to use to pay for goods, services, or debts.

In the days when money was scarce, trading was done by barter or exchange. Eggs were traded for coffee or sugar. Chickens were traded for lard or groceries or for material for a new dress. A mule could be traded for a piece of land, or a cow sold for money needed to buy the winter's supply of groceries.

Money comes to people by inheritance, by employment, by support for Christian work (preaching and missions), by welfare, and by ill-gotten ways, such as stealing, betting, gambling, bribery, selling whiskey, and pushing drugs.

Money in some form is necessary for our existence. God ordained that a man should eat of the fruit of the ground, the herb of the field (Genesis 3:17, 18): "In the sweat of thy face shalt thou eat bread" (Genesis 3:19). Therefore the honorable way to secure a livelihood is by working and taking care of the money earned. Our Lord Jesus Christ set an example by working as a carpenter (after Joseph's death) to support his mother, half brothers, and sisters until He left home to do God's work among His own people as God had ordained.

The disciples, who had left their occupation to follow Christ, had to learn that "the Lord ordained that they which preach the gospel should live of the gospel" (I Corinthians 9:14) as they launched out, trusting God to supply all their needs while they did His work. Because there are many men and women in full-time Christian work today, it is necessary that others do honest work "working with . . . [their] hands the thing which is good, that . . . [they] may have to give to him that needeth" (Ephesians 4:28).

Many years ago a young Christian man in college faced a crisis in his life soon after he had committed himself and all that he had to the Lord. He wondered whether he should reject his inheritance and a sizeable income that would be his if, after graduation, he went into his father's business. He struggled alone in his room until the assurance came that he was to be a businessman and share his income with God's people. This he did to the end of a long and prosperous life, helping to meet the financial needs of the local church, missions, and missionaries all over the world. His wedding present to his like-minded bride was a missionary, a young woman who went to China and spent many years teaching God's Word.

A recent case of self-support and sharing is a young girl who went to Camp Nathanael in the Kentucky Mountains, was saved, and gave her life to Jesus Christ. Through the help of Christian friends, she was able to get an education and special training that qualified her for a secretarial position with a good salary. A new work for Jewish people had been started, and the need for some secretarial work was met by the Kentucky girl, who helped in the evening hours.

As the work grew rapidly under God's guiding hand and blessing, a full-time secretary was needed in the office. "J" responded by offering her services at one-half the salary she had been receiving. With joy and excitement, she has related the marvelous way the Lord has worked and the thrill it has been to see Him doing the humanly impossible in the salvation and spiritual growth of all ages and types of Jewish people.

Maybe we wonder how Jesus and His disciples got along without a regular income. They were too busy those three and a half years to be able to work for their support. In Luke 8:1-3 we read that Jesus and the twelve disciples "went throughout every city and village, preaching and shewing the glad tidings of the kingdom of God." There were "certain women" and "many others" who went along and "ministered unto him of their substance." One of these women was the wife of Chuza, Herod's steward, or business manager. Certainly she was a woman of means; she had been healed by Christ (verse 2) and was a believer. So she shared her personal income with her Savior and Lord to enable Him to carry on His ministry. By her actions she said:

> Take my silver and my gold,
> Not a mite would I withhold.
> Take my love, my God, I pour
> At Thy feet its treasure store.

There are proper and improper ways to use money. The proper ways bless and the improper ones harm. The rich fool in the parable in Luke 12:16-20 hoarded his wealth for his own use and lost it in sudden death. The rich young ruler loved his money so much he could not part with it and missed the eternal life he could have had. Jesus told His disciples that it would be impossible, without God's help, for a rich man to stop loving money, to humble himself in order to enter the Kingdom of God.

Bribery is a wrong use of money. In Matthew 28:12-15 the Jewish leaders are reported as having given "large money" to the soldiers who had guarded Jesus' burying place. They were instructed to lie by saying that the disciples of Jesus had stolen His body away while they slept.

This followed closely the gift of thirty pieces of silver given by the same Jewish authorities to Judas to betray the Lord. We know the result of that bribery in the suicide of Judas. Jesus had said, " . . . it had been good for that man if he had never been born." Again in John 17:12 He called Judas the "son of perdition," who was lost. This betrayal was no sudden act of Judas. He had carried the money bag for Jesus and the other disciples and had regularly stolen from it. He loved money more than Jesus Christ, and it was the evil that destroyed him. "The love of money is the root of all evil" (I Timothy 6:10).

As Jesus hung on the cross, Roman soldiers were gambling—casting lots over his clothing, not caring that the Savior of the world, the Lord of glory, was dying in agony for their sins.

Early in His ministry, and again just before He was arrested and crucified, Jesus went into the temple at Jerusalem, overthrew the tables of the crooked money changers, and called the men thieves. They were cheating and stealing from those who were buying the items that were needed to make an offering to a holy God in praise and worship.

In the book of Acts we have the record of Ananias and Sapphira, who lied about their gifts of money; the story of Simon, the sorcerer, who tried to buy God's power with money; the account of Demetrius, the silversmith, who stirred up the silversmiths in Ephesus against Paul and his companion because he was afraid he and other silversmiths would lose their wealth; and the desire of Felix, the Roman governor, to extract a gift from Paul by hearing him often concerning his faith in Christ.

In the case of Ananias and Sapphira (Acts 5:1-10), they were struck dead immediately; in the case of Simon, the sorcerer, Peter told him, "Thy money perish with thee . . . . thy heart is not right with God" (Acts 8:18-21); in the case of Demetrius, there was great confusion and Demetrius was reprimanded by the townclerk (Acts 19:35-41); and in the case of Felix (Acts 24:24-26) the gospel messages he heard from Paul had no effect, and he remained an unsaved person headed for hell.

These examples should be enough to convince us that the love of money is indeed the root of all evil—whether it is hoarded selfishly, loved more than God; whether it is used for bribery in betraying a friend, for gambling, for cheating in business; whether it is the reason for using a place of worship to make dishonest gain, for trying to buy God's power, for lying about a gift of property; or whether it is the desire that produces fear of losing money or failing to gain political power. No wonder Jesus said in Luke 12:15, "Beware of covetousness." Where the motive is wrong, there is always the improper use of money; and only harm comes to the person who is involved. There is no blessing from God and no "treasure laid up in heaven."

Before Jesus came along and called the disciples to follow Him, they had the teaching only of the Pharisees and scribes, the religious leaders of the day. Therefore it was necessary for the Lord Jesus to tell His disciples that the Pharisees' hearts were not right with God. They taught man-made laws which had been added to the laws given by Moses; they were really hypocrites, for they did not practice what they preached.

Jesus denounced the Pharisees and scribes publicly. They pretended to be very good but were only outwardly so. They had trumpeters sounding in the streets ahead of them as they went to the temple to give their money in order to receive praise of men for their generosity, but Jesus said they "devoured widows' houses," taking the widows' money for themselves.

In the Pharisees' presence one day Jesus told the story of a certain rich man and his steward. The steward was unfaithful and had wasted his master's goods. The unjust steward made a tricky money deal, which his "boss" thought was wise. Then Jesus ended His story by saying, "No servant can serve two masters . . . . Ye cannot serve God and mammon [or money]" (Luke 16:1-13). The Pharisees who had listened derided Him because they were covetous and loved money (Luke 16:14). Jesus said, "Ye are they which justify yourselves before men, but God knoweth your hearts; for that which is highly esteemed among men is abomination in the sight of God" (Luke 16:15). Jesus exposed their hypocrisy and dishonesty in Matthew, chapter 23, saying among many other things that they were "full of extortion"; they appeared outwardly beautiful but were full of all uncleanness, hypocrisy, and iniquity. Those men were the "preachers" of that day. We as Christians are God's stewards of the possessions and money we are permitted to have. Either we will handle carefully and for His glory the money we have, or it will handle us.

To invest money wisely, in order to make more, is according to Scripture in the parable of the five, two, and one talents.

The Lord commended the two who had traded or invested the talents to double their value and condemned the one who had failed to use his one talent to put it in the hands of exchangers that the Lord would receive his own "with usury."

This illustrates the truth that all we have is from God and we are responsible to use our possessions for Him. One day we are going to give an account to Him of what we have done with our money. It is wise to take care of money in order to have more to share. To gamble on the stock market or to sign notes for others is not Christian or wise. Either of these acts can cause a man to lose all he has and make hardship for his loved ones.

A prosperous merchant in a small Kentucky town thought he would help some of his family and neighbors by signing notes to enable them to borrow from the bank. Most of them failed to pay their obligations, and the merchant because he had to meet the payments was almost wrecked financially.

Two brothers, starting as partners in a small iron and steel business in Pennsylvania at the turn of the century, agreed that they would sign no notes for anyone under any circumstances. They felt it would be better to give money direct to someone rather than jeopardize their future for themselves, their business, and their families. This worked successfully.

To give money for the Lord's work and to help the needy are the Christian's responsibility and satisfaction as expressed in some words from a familiar hymn:

> Nor should I aught withhold,
> Dear Lord, from Thee;
> In love my soul would bow,
> My heart fulfill its vow,
> Some offering bring Thee now,
> Something for Thee . . . .
> All that I am and have,
> Thy gifts so free,
> In joy, in grief, through life,
> Dear Lord, for Thee.

Jesus said in Luke 6:38, "Give, and it shall be given unto you . . . . For with the same measure that ye mete . . . it shall be measured to you again." Some people give only a tithe, which they believe is enough to give to God. Some people tithe as a bargain with God, so that He will prosper them accordingly. Some people are afraid to give liberally for fear they will have nothing to live on.

Jesus commended the widow who gave her two mites (worth one fourth of a cent in our money) to the treasury in the temple. Jesus, who knew everything about people—their motives and acts—knew it was all she had. He told the disciples she had given more than the rich people He saw putting in their gifts. They had given what they had to spare, whereas she had given all her living.

Some years ago in a Sunday school class, one of the older women argued with the teacher and some of the class members that "tithing" meant to give one-tenth of what you had left after paying all of your bills and providing for all your needs. It was hard to convince her that the Scriptures taught otherwise.

Just a short while ago a friend asked me a question about tithing. This man has been, and still is, connected with the Apollo program at Cape Kennedy. He lives in Winter Park, Florida, and belongs to a local church. He said he was confused as to where he should give his tithes, whether all of it should be given to the local church or some of it to other Christian work.

I do not remember exactly how I answered his question, but it made me think about other Christians who might have the same problem; so I decided to include my answer in this chapter.

I have known of a church where the preacher, quoting Malachi 3:10, taught the members to give all their gifts of money to the local church: "Bring ye all the tithes into the storehouse." The church members were told that the local church of their denomination was the storehouse and all their gifts of money must be given there if they were to receive a reward from the Lord. This shocked me.

When the book of Malachi was written there was only one place where a true believer in God could give his gifts to Him. That place was the house of God, the temple in Jerusalem. The same thing was true during Jesus' lifetime. Obedient Jews took their money gifts to the temple and cast (dropped) them or threw them into the treasury or collection boxes. (See Mark 12:41-44.)

On the day of Pentecost (Acts 2), when the New Testament Church began, it was—and still is—composed of all believers in Jesus Christ, those who had received Him as their Savior and Lord.

The temple in Jerusalem was destroyed in A.D. 70; so gifts of tithes and offerings could no longer be given there.

Believers in the early church and down through the centuries have given their money and possessions to keep God's work going and to meet the needs of God's people all over the known world.

Today there are many places where we can give our gifts to the Lord. A person belonging to a local church where the Gospel is preached should certainly support that church in its current expenses, missionary program, and youth work, especially if he is limited in the amount he can give to the Lord's work.

For others, like myself, who do give to our own churches, there are non-denominational organizations—such as our Scripture Memory Mountain Mission in the Kentucky Mountains, The Billy Graham Evangelistic Association, Jewish work, foreign mission societies, Christian schools and colleges—and many other places where our gifts can meet needs, be used for God's glory, and bring satisfaction and a clear conscience to us, the donors.

This is an individual matter to be decided by each person as the Holy Spirit leads. I personally like to have my money working for me all over the world.

The truth of the matter is that all we have belongs to the Lord. We should ask ourselves, "What part of it do I keep for myself?"

> We give Thee but Thine own,
> Whate'er the gift may be;
> All that we have is Thine alone,
> A trust, O Lord, from Thee.

A little girl asked her father for ten dimes in exchange for a silver dollar she had been keeping. The following Sunday she put two of the ten dimes in the church offering plate. Seeing what she had done, her father asked after church why she had put in the extra dime. She replied, "One dime belongs to the Lord as His tithe, and the other is my offering."

I attend a church in Florida where the minister says before the offering is taken, "Let us give to God His tithe and our offerings," and states that he is delighted to be the pastor of a congregation where there need be no rummage or "rubbish" sales or any gimmicks used to raise money. The people give willingly and cheerfully, and the needs of the local church and missions are met.

While we live it is a privilege to share what we have with others. "It is more blessed to give than to receive" (Acts 20:35).

An imaginative conversation was carried on between a cow and a pig. The pig said, "I'm very useful. People eat all of me, even my feet. You give only milk and some meat." "Aha," said the cow, "you give only after you are dead, but I give not only after I'm dead, but all the time I'm living."

Jesus told the disciples in Matthew 6:20, 21: "Lay not up for yourselves treasures upon earth," where they can rust or be stolen, but "lay up for yourselves treasures in heaven," where they will be safe and secure, and "there will your heart be also."

Jesus said, "A man's life consisteth not in the abundance of the things which he possesseth." The true life is not what we own, not how much money we have, but how rich we are toward God by sharing what He has given us.

A gentleman of means lived to be over ninety years of age. He was a very generous bachelor, and when he died he left nothing of any value. One young friend received a hairbrush as a memento. The man had given away all his money and had lived on income from annuities he had invested in different Christian organizations. He was rich toward God!

Christians who have means are often pursued by those who are raising money for various Christian causes. It becomes annoying and disgusting to be thought of only as a person with a bank account and a checkbook rather than as a child of God who loves to share in the Lord's work as the Holy Spirit leads.

One evening after a service at a Bible conference in Florida, the conference director (who is no longer there) invited two or three people to join his wife and him for some refreshments at a Howard Johnson's. The conversation was amazing as this man told of the wealthy people he knew and amounts of money each had, figured on their income taxes and the worth of their property. He wanted to win them to Christ, evidently hoping they would help him finance his big and expensive schemes for advancing his ministry. One of the guests was quite well-to-do and was utterly disgusted, because she was sure that he had figured what she was worth and was hoping for a large contribution. It was not given!

One Christian person who spends the winter months in Florida had to stop answering the door or the telephone because of the "hopeful tramps" who streamed through the state looking up everyone who might possibly give them a donation for their work or provide food and lodging to save expenses.

Another one always gets her checkbook ready when she knows a "regular beggar" is coming to call on her so that she can give him a small donation to get rid of him. Surely this is not God's way of meeting financial needs, for He loves a cheerful giver.

There are those Christian leaders who seem to run ahead of the Lord by building huge buildings for Christian school or church purposes or other enterprises. When the bills are due and there are no funds in hand to pay them, these individuals converge on people who are able to give substantial amounts and act as if the donor owes them the money. Sometimes they get angry or insulting when the gift is not given.

Others descend upon strangers whom they have heard of in order to secure a large sum of money. They insist upon a visit whether it is convenient or not, even though the "could-be" donor is not well. Photograph albums are produced, slides shown on the walls of the living room though unrequested; and sometimes hours are spent boring the host or hostess with information that means nothing at all to that person, who is probably wishing the visitor would hurry up and leave.

In one case a couple asked for an appointment and drove quite a distance to meet a lady they had heard of. They were told in advance that she was not well, had bad allergies, especially to paper and ink, and could see them for only a short time. Lo and behold, almost the first thing they did after arriving was to sit down on a sofa, open up and spread out large blueprints before her eyes and right under her allergic nose! They went into details of what they wanted for a very costly building. She soon had to excuse herself because the blue ink and the paper were making her deathly sick. The couple left without any donation or any encouragement for one in the future.

Later the man wrote that he was very greatly disappointed with the visit and the lack of interest on the lady's part to make a contribution, especially since he and his wife had driven a considerable distance! He must have forgotten that he had not been asked to come, that he was told in advance there would be no contribution, and that the Christian woman was not well. In fact, the visit put her in bed and hindered her from some things she was needing to do for the Lord.

These days people have their own commitments, their own daily responsibilities and interests, and do not have time to spend hours listening to long reports. There may be a few lonely people, some shut-ins or retired people who welcome a visit, but they seem to be in the minority.

An aunt of mine, who was a single lady and very generous, was visited by a "Mr. B," who told her the Lord had told him that she was to give him one thousand dollars. Being a very sensible and spiritual person, she said, "Well, the Lord works both ways and when He tells me to give it, I'll write a check and send it to you." As she was not in sympathy with his work, he did not receive her check. I have often remembered this incident and have said in my heart, "Thank you, Aunt Annie!"

One friend expressed these thoughts: "There are some Christians who give reluctantly under stress. There are some Christians who give ascetically only in order to save time. There are some who give in order to have their gifts publicized—to be made known to men. There are some Christians who give defensively because of high pressure and steam-roller tactics. These ways bring no blessing or satisfaction to the Christian, who is instructed from the Bible to give cheerfully, voluntarily from a heart filled with love for God, and as the Holy Spirit directs."

Another friend, a Christian worker who with his wife was a donor as well as a donee, expressed this: "We personally believe there are too many projects done in the energy of the flesh that could easily be curtailed until the Holy Spirit gives evidence of tangible permission. We also feel it is wrong to start a large undertaking by going around the country to try to secure the funds to carry it. This, we think, is putting the cart before the horse.

"When one of His [God's] own has a real need, the Lord honors it and will supply the need because He has promised to 'supply all [our] need according to His riches in glory by Christ Jesus' (Philippians 4:19).

"Of course, if He does not do it in this way, He may in some other way, but He will supply the need! Therefore as He is the Creator and Owner of all things, why should we have to beg men, His created beings, for the things which we need? We have access to the very source, and so, if we go to Him to make our needs known, He is able and willing to supply them."

When the Lord wants a need met, He works with the one who is to give and the one who is to receive. He will cause the needy person to ask Him, according to God's will, and will lead the one who is to give the donation to know the mind of the Spirit (Romans 8:26, 27) so that the exact amount will be given at the right time. When this happens (and it does), there is great joy on the part of each person and the satisfaction of knowing God's will has been done; and therefore His blessing will be upon the gift as it is used for eternal purposes. There are many of us who have had and are having these experiences.

An illustration of this is a gift a Christian woman was led to give to a new Jewish work some years ago. She did not know the leader of the organization but had a slight acquaintance with a member of its board of directors, whom she trusted. Her check (which she prayed about and the amount it should be) arrived at its destination on a Monday morning. At noon she received a long-distance phone call from the director of the organization, saying her check was an answer to prayer. There was no money on hand to pay the rent on their small office; and if nothing came in the mail that day, he would believe it would be God's will to give up the office and move back into his crowded home to carry on the work from there. Needless to say, he was thrilled and thankful. This has happened in other instances, according to a recent report from this man, and the blessing of God has seemed to be on this fast-growing ministry.

There is a difference between faith and presumption. "Faith" is to find God's will for His work, His way of financing it, and His time in working it all out. "Presumption" is guessing or supposing that some work is according to God's plan, plunging headlong into it, running up large bills, and then having no way of paying them.

Years ago a friend learned that lesson by taking on the responsibility of a Christian publication, personally going into debt for the large bills that were due. He quoted Romans 13:8: "Owe no man anything but to love one another"; but he said, "It's all right to go into debt for the Lord's work." This just about wrecked him financially. It took him a long time to recover from this experience. Not only did he suffer loss and embarrassment, but his loved ones suffered also.

One man wrote recently, "Yesterday morning I made a decision that in the future we would not order anything that we could not pay for in advance. When I made this decision, we had printing needs of about $150. I asked the Lord if I had made the right decision He would send in the money yesterday to pay the bill to get the material printed that was needed.

"Nothing came in yesterday morning; then nothing came in the afternoon mail either. However, the postman stopped in and said he forgot my business reply mail but would go back and pick it up and bring it to me.

"When he returned with the mail, Hallelujah, there was your gift and a check for a hundred dollars from another Christian friend! Isn't it marvelous how God leads His children to be used to accomplish His work?"

This sort of happening strengthens one's faith. It makes one realize anew there is a faithful God, who will act in money matters in a businesslike and happy way that only the Holy Spirit can accomplish as He leads His own to "ask, and it shall be given" him. And then the promise is kept: "For everyone that asketh receiveth" (Matthew 7:7, 8). We are to ask God, not man.

The convictions I have about a Christian's giving and receiving money for the Lord's work come from childhood training and many years of personal experiences.

My two brothers and I were brought up by godly parents, who taught us to give to the Lord's work from the time we had any money of our own. As income increased, especially after our parents' deaths, the ability to contribute generously became a great responsibility and pleasure. For many years we have practiced what we were taught and have found it satisfying.

An August 27, 1971, my older brother, Stewart, died of a heart attack. He was a businessman, active in civic affairs. As a Christian he had no use for any work that denied the inspiration of the Scriptures. He was very particular in seeing that his tithes and offerings went to fundamental, evangelical Christian work.

He preferred giving anonymously as Jesus taught, "Let not thy left hand know what thy right hand doeth that thine alms may be in secret." Many people and organizations were helped in this way.

However, there were those who recognized the donor. After his death a Chinese Christian lady who lives in Pennsylvania wrote to me expressing her sympathy. In her letter she said, "In 1964 we were desperately in need of financial help in order to work among the officers from Formosa, Chinese seamen and students. I tried to write five times to your brother, Stewart Huston, asking for help, but the Lord did not let me mail one of them.

"In January, 1965, to our surprise, we suddenly received a check from your brother for our work. Later he told me that he was glad that I did not write to him first. It proved to him that the Lord intended for him to help us in our service for Him.

"Ever since January, 1965, he has faithfully sent us a check every third month. Because of his interest and support I can conscientiously say that many turned to the Lord."

In our childhood home and during the lifetime of our parents, we seldom knew how much they gave or where the money went. Money was not discussed very often in our home. That was considered to be poor taste and a private matter. Many times we were conscious of those who came to our house to seek contributions. As children and young people we recognized and were "turned off" by those who attempted to "butter up" Mother and Father in order to go away with a nice, fat contribution. We liked and respected those who seemed to come for Christian fellowship out of love and admiration for our truly Christian parents.

If a person believes he is led to solicit funds for his work by giving information and has the opportunity to see a possible contributor, he should be careful about his appearance in order to be presentable, should have the right attitude, should be considerate of the person visited, and should have a personality that gives confidence to the donor.

It is better to ask outright for a gift than to hint for one. Hinting is nauseating and distasteful to some of us who want forthrightness in God's business.

The wife of a prominent, successful businessman, one who gives liberally to many causes, said it made her husband "mad" to be approached by many people who came to see him as a "friend" and then asked for a large donation or acted as if they expected one.

The fact that some people restrain themselves and appear gracious, as a Christian should, is no indication that the person is not "put out," to say the least, when valuable time is taken up.

When a gift has been acknowledged and a receipt given, it is not necessary, nor always wise, to follow it up by paying a personal call on the donor who is a busy person and has other interests. This can be quite aggravating and most inconvenient.

Thank God, there is the right method of meeting needs as well as the right use of money.

The happiest way has been mentioned before. It is to pray about the need and wait for the Lord to send in the gift or gifts in His own time and way.

However, we all need to be informed of what is going on in Christian work. That information can come from reading missionary magazines, missionary letters; hearing missionaries speak at churches or conferences; traveling and visiting various forms of Christian work.

It is wise to make an investigation of the organizations that are active for Christ in the world, those which are really making Him known. We should find out what their doctrinal statement is (what they believe and teach) and who their sponsors or members of their boards or endorsement committees are. We should check their annual financial statements to see what is their income and outgo. In other words, we should try to find out all we can about that organization to see whether it is one to which we can conscientiously give our money.

There are many interesting and varied Christian works going on all over the world that honor God by using His Word to make Christ known. There are many works that count for eternity. However, there are some that are quite the opposite! A Christian needs discernment to know the good from the bad. Corresponding with missionaries brings information and encouragement to a donor.

Just recently a missionary letter came from a young couple in West Irian, a pioneer work in a mountainous country where the people have very little of this world's goods. Returning there after a year's furlough, the missionaries were thrilled to see some of the converts carrying on the work of preaching the gospel in multiplying congregations in scattered villages. The missionary wrote: "In one valley an offering of sweet potatoes—a pile a foot high—I am told, is taken and given to the new pastor. The church here at Kiwi sends a little money offering to them also." They are giving what they have out of their poverty.

> We plow the fields and scatter
> The good seed on the land,
> But it is fed and watered

By God's almighty hand;
He sends the snow in winter,
The warmth to swell the grain,
The breezes and the sunshine,
And soft refreshing rain.

We thank Thee, then, O Father,
For all things bright and good,
The seed-time and the harvest,
Our life, our health, our food;
Accept the gifts we offer,
For all Thy love imparts,
And what Thou most desirest,
Our humble, thankful hearts.

"What is a millionaire?" a little boy asked his father one day. "A millionaire," said his father, "is a man who has a million dollars." "Then, Daddy, I'm a one-aire."

It is not the amount that counts, it is the proper spirit of giving—"not grudgingly, or of necessity; for God loveth a cheerful giver" (II Corinthians 9:7).

Give, though thy gift be small,
Still be a giver;
Out of the little fount
Proceeds the river;
Out of the river,
Gulfs soon will be
Pouring their waters out,
Making a sea.

A neighbor boy discussing with me the fact that Christmas is Jesus' birthday asked whether he should give Him a present. I replied, "I do." Then he quickly said, "How do you get it up there?" Of course, I answered, "By giving money or presents to the poor and needy and to churches and missionaries, so that the story of Jesus and His love will be told to those who have never heard."

A gift was sent to Costa Rica in Central America to complete the amount needed for the final payment on a kindergarten building that was ready to open. On the opening day a tea was given in the early afternoon for parents and interested friends. Just before the guests came, the letter, with the check enclosed, arrived. The missionary hostess who was in charge received word that the gift of $1,200 had come. Later, she wrote that she was "so excited and so grateful" she "couldn't eat any of the refreshments. Getting that news before the tea and knowing that all our needs and more were met made the Lord's presence and goodness seem very, very near. I have to keep reminding myself that God's love that sometimes withholds is the same love that gives. The Scripture reading for the service was Matthew 7:7-12 about asking and receiving and getting good gifts from the heavenly Father."

This letter brought joy to the one who was led to give the money and to the one who received it.

Those who love money more than they love God are too numerous. Even Christians fail in this matter. As one has written from experience, "Sometimes there are Christians who miss God's best for themselves because of love for money and things."

This is sad when we have only one life to live. Here is where the love of money, that can buy things, is robbing an individual and God's people of tremendous blessing. The fullness of blessing has been missed.

We have God's Word to speak to our hearts; God's Son, who gave His all, to be our example; and God's Holy Spirit to guide us in our decisions.

Down through the centuries and in our changing world today, we have the testimonies of many Christians who know the results of giving God's way.

The "recipe" is found in II Corinthians 8:1-5, where it is recorded that the Macedonian churches gave beyond their power, willingly, joyfully, first giving their own selves to the Lord and to those to whom the gift was given. This made it very personal— from a personal God, through the Christian, a person, to other persons with love.

A 1970 recipe has been given upon request from the director of a non-denominational mission in the Kentucky Mountains:

"I first heard about living by faith when still a teen-ager. Now twenty-five years later, having served the Lord in full-time Christian work for almost twenty years, I have come to some definite conclusions:

1. *Talk to the Lord about financial needs.* This is my responsibility. The Lord has proven to honor the first approach. When needs are met, I know that those who have given are led of the Holy Spirit and not by persuasion.

2. *Practice giving.* My wife and I believe in and practice giving at least twenty per cent of our income to the Lord's work.

3. *Live within the budget.* This includes the type of housing, automobile, food, clothing, and vacation. Needed items should be purchased only when money is available. Credit and carrying charges should be avoided. I have observed that those who always talk and write about needs are those who always seem to have needs. Many times they are heavily in debt, having purchased non-essentials.

4. *Never doubt the Lord's provision for every need.*"

Scriptural Uses of Money

1.	Support your family.	I Timothy 5:8
2.	Support your minister and missionaries.	I Timothy 5:18
		I Corinthians 9:14
3.	Support the weak.	Acts 20:35
4.	Pay your taxes.	Romans 13:1, 6, 7
		Matthew 22:21
5.	Pay your bills.	Romans 13:8
6.	Contribute to poor Christians.	Romans 15:26
7.	Give generously.	II Corinthians 9:6
8.	Give with purpose of heart (love) cheerfully.	II Corinthians 9:7
9.	Give with simplicity.	Romans 12:8
10.	Give quietly and secretly.	Matthew 6:3
11.	Realize the personal choice—the money is yours.	Matthew 20:15
12.	Give for eternity.	Matthew 6:20
13.	Give not for self but to God.	Matthew 22:21
14.	Give in order to give a good account.	Romans 14:12
15.	Give to receive a reward (Moses—Hebrews 11:24-26).	I Corinthians 3:12-14
16.	Give willingly from what you have.	II Corinthians 8:12

17.	Give from poverty or from abundance.	II Corinthians 8:2, 14
18.	Give systematically and regularly.	I Corinthians 16:1, 2
19.	Prepare your gifts in advance.	II Corinthians 9:4, 5
20.	Flee the love of money as one of "these things."	I Timothy 6:10, 11

Do not	be deceived by riches,	Mark 4:18, 19
	trust in riches,	I Timothy 6:17, 19
	covet riches,	I Timothy 6:10
	suppose gain is godliness.	I Timothy 6:5

Do	" . . . follow after righteousness, godliness, faith, love, patience, meekness."	I Timothy 6:11

"Godliness with contentment is great gain."   I Timothy 6:6

CHAPTER SEVEN

Toward

Pleasure—God's Presence

Thou wilt shew me the path of life: in thy presence is fulness of joy; at thy right hand there are pleasures for evermore" (Psalm 16:11). There are three words in this verse we should read and think about in this chapter: "Presence," "Joy," "Pleasures."

David, the man who wrote and sang this 16th Psalm, was a happy man, probably one of the happiest in the Old Testament record. He was not only a shepherd boy and a king of Israel, but was "the sweet psalmist of Israel" (II Samuel 23:1).

David loved music. He composed and sang psalms and invented musical instruments (Amos 6:5). He was the organizer of an orchestra that played with psalteries and harps, cymbals and trumpets. He appointed certain men "to record" his words as he delivered to Asaph and his brethren a psalm of thanksgiving to the Lord (I Chronicles 16:4-8). Later when he made his son Solomon king of Israel, David chose a choir of four thousand men to sing and praise the Lord with the instruments he, David, had made (I Chronicles 23:5).

"David and all the house of Israel played before the Lord on all manner of instruments made of fir wood [cypress], even on harps, and on psalteries, and on timbrels, and on cornets, and on cymbals" (II Samuel 6:5). Do you know that a psaltery, or viol, was an instrument of six, eight, or ten strings plucked with fingers like a guitar? It was played to accompany a voice. It was an ancient instrument. Did you know that the harp was the national instrument of the Hebrews? There were two sizes: some with eight strings and some with ten.

105

Other instruments mentioned in I Samuel 10:5 are a tabret and a pipe. Do you know that a "tabret" is another name for "timbrel," a sort of tambourine played by women? A pipe, or flute, was one of the simplest and oldest of musical instruments. Shepherds played their pipes thousands of years ago. The pipe was probably used by David as he tended sheep on the hillsides below Bethlehem.

For those of us who love music—play instruments or sing—we know how much pleasure it gives to us and, we hope, to others. It is nice to know that musicians were honored throughout the Bible history and that the men who furnished the orchestra and choruses for worship stood next to the kings and priests in prestige.

David was a "cunning player on a harp," so much so that when he played before King Saul the evil spirit in Saul departed and the king was refreshed by David's music.

According to the dictionary a "psalm" is a "song sung to the harp" or "a sacred song or hymn." David sang: "Praise the Lord with harp: sing unto him with the psaltery and an instrument of ten strings. Sing unto him a new song; play skilfully with a loud noise" (Psalm 33:2, 3). This was joyful music with the right motive—unto the Lord. David believed in playing "skilfully," doing his very best for his God.

What is "pleasure"? It is "a pleased feeling, enjoyment, delight, satisfaction, joy, fun, gladness, to be made happy or make happy."

I am sure David experienced these sensations at various times in his life because he could sing the 104th Psalm and bless the Lord for His greatness in creation—the God who

Stretched out the heavens like a curtain;
Laid the beams of His chambers in the waters,
Laid the foundations of the earth;
Covered the earth with waters above the mountains;
Uncovered the mountains and valleys;
Caused rivers and springs to flow in valleys and among hills for an adequate water supply for the maintenance of life;
Made trees for birds, grass for cattle, herbs and seeds for man, and bread which strengthens man's heart;
Made high hills as refuge for goats;
Made rocks for conies (badgers);

106

Made the moon for seasons, the sun for daylight, the darkness
for beasts of prey to find food and dens for places of rest;

Made the great and wide sea with innumerable great and small
creatures all dependent upon God for the food which they
needed and which He provided.

The psalmist recognized God's power in creation as he sang, "O
LORD, how manifold are thy works! in wisdom hast thou made
them all: the earth is full of thy riches" (verse 24).

Then in verses 33 and 34 he shows his feeling of pleasure in all
that God has done: "I will sing unto the Lord as long as I live: I
will sing praise to my God while I have my being. My meditation
of him shall be sweet: I will be glad in the Lord."

David knew where the sun and moon came from and why they
are here (Psalm 104:19-24). He believed the record in Genesis
1:14-18 of God's creating them for His purposes.

For David there were clean air to breathe, pure water to drink,
unpolluted land to enjoy. Generations before David was born, God
had told Joshua to drive out the enemies who possessed this land
of Canaan and to return to "the land of your possession" and
enjoy it. Centuries later David, the shepherd boy, could also enjoy
that land as he sat on a hillside near Bethlehem playing his harp
and singing. It was a lovely land—a perfect environment for men,
beasts, and birds to live in. There was harmony and balance in
nature—the "ecology" that is so often spoken of today.

David could delight in this land as he said, "The lines are fallen
unto me in pleasant places." David found pleasure in what he saw
around him. This was his country, his world that God had made.
He believed that what the Creator had made was very good
(Genesis 1:31) and that for God's pleasure all things were made
and created (Revelation 4:11). David believed that "the works of
the Lord are great, sought out of all them that have pleasure
therein" (Psalm 111:2).

As David led his father's flocks into green pastures and beside
the still waters, he knew the Lord was his Shepherd and would
lead him in paths of righteousness, and he, David, would dwell in
the house of the Lord forever.

David, the man after God's own heart, was chosen by God to be
the king of Israel not for his outward appearance (I Samuel 16:7),
although he was handsome (verse 12), but because of "the
integrity of his heart" (Psalm 78:70-72).

107

God knew David would love Him and love His people and could be trusted with a great responsibility.

At an early age David learned to know and love God personally. He could sing: "The Lord is my shepherd . . . . He maketh me to lie down . . . he leadeth me . . . . He restoreth my soul . . . . I will fear no evil: for thou art with me [God's presence] . . . . my cup runneth over [overflowing joy]."

David early learned to trust God. When a lion and a bear came to take a lamb out of his flock, he killed them. With his faith in God this experience gave him the courage to defy the giant Goliath and in the name of the Lord of Hosts to kill him.

David was a success as a shepherd boy: he loved his sheep and protected them.

David was a success as a warrior: he loved his country and won many battles.

David was a success as a king: he loved his people and was popular, for "whatsoever the king did pleased all the people" (II Samuel 3:36).

David was a man of wealth and had a large family: he dearly loved his children.

David had many friends, especially Jonathan, who loved him and whom he loved.

All of these things must have brought pleasure, for every person enjoys success and popularity.

Even though David had everything a human heart could desire, he discovered that the place of true joy was in the presence of God. He could talk to God in prayer, sing praises to Him, tell God of his feelings for Him: "I love the Lord, because he hath heard my voice and my supplications. I will walk before the Lord in the land of the living" (Psalm 116:1, 9). But David knew he could be fully satisfied only when he would behold God's face in righteousness and would be like him (Psalm 17:15). Then he would have "pleasures for evermore."

God found David, the son of Jesse, to be a "man after mine own heart which shall fulfill all my will" (Acts 13:22); and David did just that, except in the mistake he made with Bathsheba, the wife of Uriah. We know that David lost his joy through this sinful act; for when he acknowledged and confessed his sin, he asked

God: "Restore unto me the joy of thy salvation" (Psalm 51:12). David found temporary pleasure with this beautiful woman, but remorse afterwards; and he paid for this sin in his family.

There is pleasure in sin, but it does not satisfy.

Another Old Testament character, Moses, knew something of "the pleasures of sin" in Egypt. Surely, at the age of forty, Moses as the adopted son of Pharaoh's daughter had seen all the excitement, wealth, and pleasures of life in a palace. The luxury, priceless treasures, architectural beauty and every sort of entertainment, gay parties, fun, good food, wine, beautiful women, beautiful clothes, meeting important people from all over the known world, culture, art, travel, and a bright future in an idolatrous country—all became "pleasures of sin" to Moses (Hebrews 11:24-27).

Suddenly he made a choice. He refused to be called the son of Pharaoh's daughter, to enjoy the pleasures of sin any longer, and left, forsaking Egypt, giving up all prospects of a wonderful future to endure a hard life with his own people, the people of God. He looked forward to an eternal home with Christ and spiritual rewards. Therefore he refused to worship idols and "kept the passover" (Hebrews 11:28), identifying himself with the Hebrews in their God-given worship, the sacrifice of a lamb—the picture of Christ who was to come.

How could Moses endure this drastic change in his manner of living? He did "as seeing him who is invisible," who promised, "Certainly I will be with thee"; "My presence shall go with thee and I will give thee rest." Here was the secret of Moses' success: God's presence with him. He did the humanly impossible task of securing freedom from Egypt for his people and leading them for forty years in the wilderness. Moses obeyed step by step and went up to the top of Mt. Sinai to receive God's law written on tablets. Moses was there for forty days and forty nights. This was an awesome experience for Moses as he talked with God, but not a fearful one. Imagine having a forty-day conference with God in person! It was wonderful! Moses' face was so shiny from the light and joy of God's presence that it had to be covered with a veil before the people could look at him.

What did God's presence bring to Moses? It brought joy, peace, and all the blessings of knowing God personally—a God of great love and goodness. What a contrast that was to the early life of feasting and drinking, sex, dancing, and every activity of a heathen court which was all for selfish purposes, but never satisfying continually.

What a joy it must have been, and what a delight and gladness Moses must have felt at the Red Sea when God used him to perform the miracle of deliverance! Later on Moses must have been pleased and made humbly happy when, after finishing the tedious work of making the tabernacle according to God's pattern, the cloud covered it all, and the glory of the Lord filled the tabernacle or "tent of meeting." Here was God's presence evident not only to Moses, but also to all his people, because God's plan had been perfectly carried out.

Moses was faithful and obedient to God in all but the act of striking the rock for water, instead of speaking to it as God had commanded. Because of this act he was not permitted to enter the promised land. Yet he was "faithful in all his house, as a servant" (Hebrews 3:5) and God often called him "my servant Moses."

How satisfying and delightful it must have been centuries later to meet the glorified Christ on the mountain in the land of promise and to talk with Him about future events! What an honor this was to God's servant! What a pleased feeling Moses must have had in his heart!

Moses and David lived long, successful lives in fellowship with their Lord, enjoying His presence and loving care; but there was a man who enjoyed the Lord's nearness for three hundred years. That man was Enoch.

We know very little about Enoch, one of the most ancient men in the Bible. What we do know is very interesting. He was the seventh generation from Adam (Jude 14). Adam lived to be 930 years old (Genesis 5:5). Enoch's father, Jared, lived to be 962 years old (Genesis 5:20). The four men who came between Adam and Jared each lived over or just under 900 years. Enoch's son Methuselah lived to be 969 years old (Genesis 5:27); yet Enoch, at the age of 365 years, a young age for those days, was translated without death to be in God's presence.

At the age of sixty-five Enoch had become the father of Methuselah, his first son (Genesis 5:21). "And Enoch walked with God after he begat Methuselah three hundred years and begat sons and daughters" (verse 22). "And Enoch walked with God; and he was not; for God took him." One day Enoch suddenly disappeared "and was not found, because God had translated him" (Hebrews 11:5).

As Enoch walked with God we are told in Jude, verses 14 and 15, that Enoch prophesied of future judgment to come upon all ungodly people for their deeds and speeches against God.

Here was a husband, a father, a neighbor, a citizen, and a preacher who walked with God for three hundred years. Think of the influence of such a man on his generation!

Enoch's influence on Methuselah, his oldest son, by example, counsel, and instruction affected future generations. This was according to God's plan and commands—that fathers should tell their children of the Lord's "strength and wonderful works." The children were to pass this testimony on to their children that the generation to come might know God's commands and keep them. (See Psalm 78:1-7.)

Methuselah must have passed this word on to his son Lamech, who in turn instructed Noah, his son, for Noah was the only man on earth in his day who "found grace in the eyes of the Lord," who "was a just man and perfect in his generations" and who "walked with God" (Genesis 6:8, 9).

"The Lord looketh from heaven; he beholdeth all the sons of men. Behold, the eye of the Lord is upon them that fear him, upon them that hope in his mercy" (Psalm 33:13, 18). As God looked on the earth His eye beheld Noah, Enoch's great-grandson, walking uprightly alone with Him in a time of violence and wickedness, and it was because of Noah's fearing Him and hoping in His mercy that God rescued the human race from destruction.

Three generations before Noah was born, the Lord had looked from heaven and had seen Enoch walking with Him by faith, loving and obeying Him, praying without ceasing, preaching to warn sinners of judgment to come and trusting Him in all things. "But without faith it is impossible to please him [God]" (Hebrews 11:6). Enoch had the kind of faith that pleased God, that gave God pleasure; so God took him to heaven to enjoy His presence forever (Hebrews 11:5). God—a God of love—wanted the one who loved Him close to Him where He was.

We are not told exactly why God "took" Enoch at the prime of his life, but we are sure Enoch's work on earth was finished, his time had come, and God wanted him in heaven.

Enoch met the qualifications of true faith. He believed that God was real, and he diligently sought Him. God's presence gave Enoch pleasure, for Enoch enjoyed God, and Enoch's life was satisfactory to God.

Is your life satisfactory to God? Is mine? It should be. We should be able to say with the song writer:

> Breathe on me, Breath of God,
> Fill me with life anew,
> That I may love what Thou dost love,
> And do what Thou wouldst do.

There is a man in the New Testament who wrote about Jesus Christ: "Whom . . . ye love; in whom . . . ye rejoice with joy unspeakable." This was Peter, the fisherman, who left his fishing to follow Christ. Probably the thing Peter enjoyed most in life was fishing. He said when wanting something to do, "I go a fishing." He must have loved his days on the Sea of Galilee catching fish.

Peter made a wise choice when he left fishing to follow Jesus, for he had the privilege of being on the mountain when Moses and Elijah came to talk to Jesus about His decease soon to happen near Jerusalem. Here was such a delightful experience Peter, though frightened by the unusual and strange sight, said to Jesus, "Master, it is good for us to be here." This was it! and he wanted nothing else but to stay right there in the presence of the glorified Christ. This was more fun than catching fish. Think what he would have missed if he had not followed Christ.

What about Saul of Tarsus before his conversion? He must have enjoyed his life as a Pharisee. With his excellent background of family heritage, culture, education, prestige, and knowledge of Jewish law, he had a full and interesting life.

The sports and games of those days must have appealed to him. He wrote about running a race, receiving a prize, training or disciplining his body, pressing toward the mark for the prize, fighting a good fight, finishing the course, receiving the victor's crown.

And yet none of these things meant anything to him when Jesus Christ revealed Himself to Saul (later called Paul) and called him to a life of suffering and hardship.

Paul counted all former pleasures as refuse (trash) in comparison with belonging to Christ and knowing Him.

At one time all of his companions became afraid and deserted him, but he wrote: " . . . the Lord stood with me and strengthened me" (II Timothy 4:16, 17). The presence of the Lord that day was worth more than all of his companions. No wonder he could write to the Christians at Philippi (and to us): "Rejoice in the Lord alway; and again I say, Rejoice."

These five men—David, Moses, and Enoch in the Old Testament and Peter and Paul in the New Testament—were different from one another in many ways. Each one, however, had at least one thing in common: he knew God personally; he talked and walked with God on earth; he loved and served God. For a time each man knew the wonder and joy of having the presence of God with him. Each man knew human pleasure and success; each man allowed God to choose his path of life; each man was strengthened by God; each man knew that human pleasures are temporary and do not satisfy; and each looked forward to "pleasures for evermore." But not one of these five men was perfect. Only one perfect man ever lived on the earth, Jesus Christ, God's Son.

As the perfect Son of God, a human being with normal desires, Jesus declared to the scribes and Pharisees in John 8:29: "He that sent me is with me; the Father hath not left me alone; for I do always those things that please him." Here was the secret of Jesus' life: always doing the things that pleased God, continually having the presence of God with Him.

Because Jesus always pleased God by obeying Him, He could say at Lazarus' grave: "Father, I thank thee that thou hast heard me. And I knew that thou hearest me always" (John 11:41, 42). God's presence with Him always, God answering His prayers always—what greater joy could there be!

What could Jesus enjoy, or find pleasure in, while on earth?

1. As a boy, talking with the doctors in Jerusalem about spiritual things.
2. His friends, His disciples. He loved to be with them.
3. Social life—a wedding at Cana; supper at Bethany, at Emmaus, at Zacchaeus' home.
4. Talking with individuals about eternal matters—Nicodemus, the Samaritan woman, and others.

5. Little children.
6. Preaching and teaching.
7. Feeding the hungry multitudes.
8. Controlling the winds and the waves with God's power.
9. Helping people—healing them from all sorts of diseases.
10. Being alone on the mountain in prayer to His Father.

Why did Jesus enjoy these things? He was known as "a man of sorrows and acquainted with grief," yet he could say to His disciples in John 15:11, "These things have I spoken unto you, that my joy might remain in you." Later in John 17:13, He asked God "that they [believers] might have my joy fulfilled in themselves." Jesus had joy in Him because He did God's will. Jesus loved God and enjoyed doing His will. Even the agony of the cross could be endured with inner joy "for the joy that was set before him" (Hebrews 12:2). And what was the "joy" that was set before Him? Jesus looked forward to that day when He would be able to present those whom He had redeemed faultless before the presence of God's glory with exceeding joy (Jude 24). They would be His love-gift to His Father.

What about Christians today? There are certainly "pleasures of sin" to be shunned.

A missionary was traveling in a Moslem country. He felt he should witness of Jesus to a Moslem fellow-passenger. The Moslem then tried to "entertain" the missionary with what he enjoyed: tales of immorality among the passengers on board the ship. The missionary had to stop the Moslem by saying that he was not amused. He told the Moslem he needed Christ to free his heart from the love of gossiping about sinful pleasures.

Later on in his travels the same missionary met a Chinese who wanted to show him some sexy pictures in a movie magazine. The Chinese man thought them entertaining, but the missionary in disgust hit the page with his fist and tore the paper.

A bit later, someone else gave the missionary a book written by a celebrated author and told him he ought to read it. The book was well written but full of lurid descriptions of adulterous acts; so it was flung, unfinished by the missionary, into the ocean.

Quite recently there was on television an interview with the author of a book called *The Pleasure Seekers*. We were told that the young people start hunting for pleasure with tobacco and alcohol and then go on to marijuana, LSD, and heroin. These young people are yielding to the pressures of those who are pushing the sale of drugs to make a fortune. They believe they will find satisfaction in these "pleasures," but one cigarette leads to another, one drink leads to another, and smoking "pot" leads on to the most dangerous drug of all—heroin. The tragedy is that no lasting satisfaction can be found in these temporary "pleasures" but only slavery to a harmful habit.

A famous man once said he would make a fortune if he could manufacture and sell a pill that would assure the persons who swallowed it continual happiness for the rest of their lives. To be able to escape suffering and unpleasantness, people would do almost anything.

The Lord Jesus on the cross refused to drink vinegar mixed with gall (myrrh), a stupefying drink that would ease the intense suffering of the crucifixion. He went through the awful agony with a clear mind to do God's will (Matthew 26:42; Luke 22:42, 44), to empty the full cup of suffering for humanity in order that men might be delivered from eternal suffering.

Only through and in Christ can anyone—young people included—find freedom and satisfaction, which cannot be found in drugs.

> My Jesus, I love Thee, I know Thou art mine,
> For Thee all the follies of sin I resign.

What are "follies"? They are "a lack of understanding, a lack of sense or rational conduct; being silly, senseless, foolish." In Mark 7:22 Jesus said that "foolishness" is one of the evil things that come from within a man and defile him. It is just plain foolish to form habits that wreck a person's health and enslave him.

What can Christians enjoy? So far in this book we have answers in previous chapters: Christians can enjoy the Bible (Chapter One), fellowship with God (Chapter Two), victory over self (Chapter Three), winning the lost (Chapter Four), lawful possessions (Chapter Five), and the blessing of sharing one's money (Chapter Six). And in Chapter Seven we find that Christians can enjoy the constant presence of God.

We are not to be "lovers of pleasure more than lovers of God" (II Timothy 3:4). Paul said in I Thessalonians 4:1 that a Christian's walk (daily conduct) should "please God."

115

On "This Is Your Life" TV program, Ralph Edwards recently made the comment, "Happy people are those who make other people happy." This is absolutely true. To give pleasure is much more "fun" than to get it. To know we have pleased God should give us more pleasure than anything else.

We are going to please Him through all eternity, so why not start now?

What can all ages of Christians enjoy? We can enjoy music as David did. A musical instrument played skillfully by an artist, such as Van Cliburn or Heifetz, or a full orchestra producing thrilling, beautifully played music can give great pleasure to the listeners and musicians alike. The singing of those with gifted, well-trained voices can bring delight to an audience of music lovers and a pleased feeling to those who have sung their very best.

The best music of the world may please our senses, but it cannot compare with that of a congregation singing together from the heart such a hymn as "How Great Thou Art."

When singing sacred music alone or with any group, we must beware of letting our thoughts center on how our voice sounds, how well we are singing our part, how we look to others (and we are all guilty of mind-wandering) or of anything else that will keep us from thinking of the meaning of the words we are singing. It takes a great deal of concentration and heart desire to sing with understanding and praise to God words that we honestly believe and mean. If we succeed in doing this, God is pleased and so are we.

Young Christians can find true pleasure in "rock" music if it honors Jesus Christ and is sung or played naturally and from the heart. A group of Christian teen-agers spent several days one summer in the mountains of Kentucky. Their appearance, their antics, and unnatural actions as they sang their folk music were so conspicuous that many of us who were trying to listen did not hear one word they were singing. The whole effect was negative and the purpose of their performance failed, if their intent was to glorify Christ.

When we can go somewhere, do something, sing or say something, see something, be with someone and feel that we are pleasing God and that His presence is with us, then we know we are doing what is right.

We can enjoy some of the wonder and beauty of God's creation as David did. There are still unspoiled, unpolluted places in the world to be seen and enjoyed: beautiful mountains, the restless ocean, lovely lakes, streams, the canyons of the western part of the United States, and the islands of the sea, as well as many more spots in other parts of the world. When we know the Creator, such scenery makes us praise Him for His greatness.

Two men who with their wives were house guests at different times expressed delight at the crystal clear water, nearly one hundred per cent pure, that flows from the Silver Springs in Florida. A teen-aged guest found her pleasure in gazing out over the wild, free ocean at Daytona Beach. The Smoky Mountains in Tennessee and North Carolina, when seen at their best (free from crowds), have always brought delight and refreshing to those of us who love mountains.

If we like the creatures God has made and cannot find them in their natural habitat, we can see and enjoy them in such places as The Parrot Jungle, The Seaquarium, and Busch Gardens in Florida. A lively five-year-old stood for over half an hour fascinated and entranced by the antics of trained macaws and cockatoos at Busch Gardens. Another boy, a lively four-year-old, loved seeing the feeding of sharks in an open canal at the Seaquarium and was not a bit afraid.

Lovely flowers please many of us. They still can be found growing in their natural environment in many places of the world or can be enjoyed, for instance, at Cypress Gardens, in the Sarasota Jungle Gardens in Florida, as well as in private gardens which are open to the public, such as Longwood Gardens near Wilmington, Delaware.

The good things God has placed on earth should mean more to a Christian than to a person who has never received Christ. In the words from a hymn:

> Heaven above is softer blue,
> Earth around is sweeter green,
> Something lives in every hue,
> Christless eyes have never seen;
> Birds with gladder songs o'erflow,
> Flowers with deeper beauty shine,
> Since I know as now I know
> I am His and He is mine.

Some other things to enjoy are these:

1. Seeing God work when we have obeyed Him as Moses did
2. Walking with God among family and friends as Enoch did
3. Fishing for men as Peter did
4. Traveling and preaching the gospel as Paul did, reading books (he wrote to Timothy to bring him books), writing letters to missionaries and Christians needing encouragement (more than half of the New Testament Epistles were written by Paul), and having fellowship with many Christian friends as he did

Paul knew what refreshing from other Christians meant, for he wrote of the "joy of Titus" when he was "refreshed" by the Corinthian Christians (II Corinthians 7:13).

There are no nicer friends on earth than like-minded Christians, who love Jesus Christ first. To have fellowship with them brings a taste of heaven to earth and gives refreshing (or "fun") such as worldly people without Christ cannot possibly have.

What about sports, games, swimming, Hondas, TV, books, magazines, and movies that teen-agers especially enjoy? The answer depends upon the motive and the after-effect. If we can do these things for the glory of God—to have good exercise and relaxation, to be entertained or better informed, to make good friends and to feel the closeness of Christ during and after the "pleasures" are over—we can feel free to do them, but usually in moderation.

God wants us to have joy in our lives—His joy, Christ's joy. The good things in life can be enjoyed if they honor Him and are for our good. An occupation and secular work well done bring satisfaction and a sense of enjoyment to a Christian. If we can take Jesus with us in all we do and feel His presence and His pleasure in our activities, then we can know that the fun and work are all right. If something seems to be wrong and Jesus is not near or pleased, then we should go to Him and ask the reason why.

> Earthly pleasures vainly call me;
> I would be like Jesus.[2]

And what was Jesus like? He went where people were. He always pointed them to God. He spoke God's words and did God's works. His pleasure was in doing God's will, in being in God's presence, in spending hours in prayer to His Father.

I have tried to emphasize the words "presence, joy, and pleasures" throughout this chapter because of their power in our daily lives made possible by Christ, who lives within us.

Many years ago I went on a cruise to the Holy Land. Although I was a Christian, I had never felt very close to the Lord. One afternoon as I stood with a group of Christians beside the Sea of Galilee, a boat came toward us, rowed by fishermen in native garb. As the boat came close to shore, one man jumped into the water to pull the bow of the boat onto dry land. Then each fisherman took hold of the net and stretched it out, looking for tears and rips to mend. We watched in silence for a few minutes until someone in the crowd started singing:

> As of old apostles heard Him
> By the Galilean Lake,
> Turned from home, and toil, and kindred
> Leaving all for His dear sake.

Suddenly I realized that I, Ruth Huston, was standing on ground that Jesus, the Son of God, might have walked on when He was here on earth. For the first time in my life I felt His presence come to me as if He were actually there. The effect was humbling, and brought a deep sense of joy. The tears were hard to keep back and I have never been the same since. That presence brought warmth, comfort, love, strength, security, and a desire to live wholly for Him until that day when He takes me home.

We can look forward as David did to the "pleasures for evermore"; but, you know, just as we have eternal life now because Christ is in us, so can we have eternal pleasures now, as well as in heaven. We are seated in heavenly places in Christ (Ephesians 1:3). He is at God's right hand and our pleasures are in Him. We do not have to wait until we get to heaven to be happy. We can enjoy eternal life here now and "pleasures for evermore."

Some people feel they cannot be happy until they get to heaven, but that is not true.

> Friends all around me are trying to find
> What the heart yearns for, by sin undermined;

I have this secret, I know where 'tis found;
Only true pleasures in Jesus abound.
All that I want is in Jesus,
He satisfies, joy He supplies,
Life would be worthless without Him,
All things in Jesus I find.[3]

The best the world has to offer of lawful pleasure is nothing compared to day-by-day fellowship with Jesus Christ. "In thy presence is fulness of joy." If you do not have this as a Christian, why not try it? It is the best cure there is for loneliness.

To start the day with Him in prayer, to walk through the hours with the awareness that He is with and in us, and to "pray without ceasing [constant communication]" can make an exciting experience of what might otherwise be a dull day.

In John 16:24 Jesus told His disciples to ask God for things in His name: " . . . ask, and ye shall receive, that your joy may be full."

A neighbor, an older woman who hated housework, found herself one morning without a maid. The maid had left for good. My neighbor dreaded what was ahead. Suddenly it occurred to her that as a Christian she could ask the Lord's help. After three hours of hard, unaccustomed work, she was amazed at how the time had flown by, how easy the work had been, and how much had been accomplished. Very joyfully she said, "Thank you, Lord."

The tests for us are these: What do we really enjoy? Whom do we like to be with? Do we enjoy the things that please God? "Man's chief end is to glorify God and *enjoy Him* forever." That means now, on earth, as well as throughout eternity in heaven.

What can we enjoy according to God's Word? We can have:

1. Joy in God (a Person) through Jesus Christ (Romans 5:11)
2. Joy of hearing that sinners have repented and are saved (Luke 15:7)
3. Joy of faith (Philippians 1:25)
4. Joy of speaking "face to face" with Christians we love (II John 12)
5. Joy of hearing that believers are walking in truth, acting like Christians (III John 4)

6. Joy of knowing we have pleased God (Hebrews 13: 15, 16) by praising Him with our lips, doing good, and sharing what we have with others

The fruit of the Spirit is "joy" (Galatians 5:22).

I Peter 1:8—believing with joy (saving faith)
I Peter 4:13—exceeding joy (better than any other kind)
Matthew 2:10—exceeding great joy at Jesus' birth (the real Christmas spirit)
II Corinthians 8:2—abundance of joy (through sharing with others)
John 15:11—fullness of joy (His joy by abiding in His love)
John 16:20, 22—the joy of His resurrection (Jesus said, "Your heart shall rejoice, and your joy no man taketh from you.")
Matthew 28:8—the great joy (with which the women departed from the empty tomb.)

Do we delight in a risen, living Savior? We should.

The minister of a church that was packed full for the Easter morning service told his audience, after the singing by the choir of a joyful Easter anthem, that, unknown to them, he had been watching many of their faces. He was looking to see how many people were believing and responding to the message of joy they were hearing. Some looked sleepy; some looked as if they had been made to come to church and were bored. He was glad to see the faces of those who showed evidence that they were responding from their hearts to this marvelous message of the resurrection of the Lord Jesus Christ from the dead.

Free from themselves, their problems, their daily tasks, those people looked as if they were "lost in wonder, love, and praise."

> Love divine, all loves excelling,
> Joy of heaven to earth come down . . . .
> Thee we would be always blessing,
> Serve Thee as Thy hosts above,
> Pray, and praise Thee without ceasing,
> Glory in Thy perfect love . . . .
> Till in heav'n we take our place,
> Till we cast our crowns before Thee,
> Lost in wonder, love, and praise.

121

CHAPTER EIGHT

Toward

Circumstances—God's Providence

In the life of every Christian, circumstances play a large part. "Circumstances" are "occurrences, happenings, events, things that come to pass," that turn up in our lives, that arise and befall us human beings. "Providence" is "the benevolent guidance of God for people and in nature."

The apostle Paul knew by experience the words he wrote to the Christians at Rome: "And we know that all things [happenings] work together for good to them that love God, to them who are the called according to his purpose" (Romans 8:28).

Paul also learned that God's purpose in hardship and suffering was that he should "be conformed to the image [or character]" of Christ (Romans 8:29).

Do you know any Christian who has gone through more unusual and difficult circumstances than the apostle Paul?

When Ananias expressed fear of Saul, the Pharisee (Acts 9:13, 14), the Lord said, "Go thy way: for he is a chosen vessel unto me, to bear my name before the Gentiles, and kings, and the children of Israel: For I will show him how great things he must suffer for my name's sake" (Acts 9:15, 16). These words of the Lord came true as Paul witnessed to Felix, Festus, King Agrippa, the children of Israel, and the Gentiles. With it all came the promised suffering.

Paul often experienced rejection of his witness for Christ. Rejection is hard for anyone, especially when the Lord Jesus is not wanted by those we love, pray for, or witness to.

Paul listed some of his trials in II Corinthians 4:8, 9; 6:4-10; 11:23-28. These all came to pass as he did God's will.

Yet he spoke of our "light affliction, which is but for a moment" (II Corinthians 4:17), and the "far more exceeding and eternal weight of glory" which the momentary affliction was working out for Paul and his companions. (Notice that the word "weight" is on the glory side and the word "affliction," in comparison, is called "light.") It is good for Christians to be afflicted. We should welcome affliction!

Paul told us in II Corinthians 4:18 how to go through hard things. We are to look "at the things which are not seen"—which "are eternal." We are to look quickly to Jesus! He, Paul, found that "the things which happened unto me have fallen out rather unto the furtherance of the gospel" (Philippians 1:12), and he could truly write, "I am exceeding joyful in all our tribulation" (II Corinthians 7:4).

The Lord can be our "strength and song" as Moses and the children of Israel sang after deliverance from the humanly impossible circumstances at the Red Sea (Exodus 15:1, 2).

Years ago I found this to be true in my own experience. One day I was appointed to be in charge of a meeting. Just five minutes before the meeting began, a sudden, unexpected, upsetting thing happened that made me wonder whether I could possibly go through with my responsibility. There was just time enough for me to duck into a nearby empty room, get down on my knees before a chair, and ask the Lord for His help. Immediately, all nervousness and weakness were replaced by marvelous strength and a song in my heart that helped me through the trying circumstance with a smile on my face and a new experience of God's triumphing in my life.

What about Moses? Who had a longer, more varied life with difficulties than he, who, at eighty years of age, started leading all those complaining, disobedient Israelites from Egypt to the Promised Land? But his help came from God, who said, "My presence shall go with thee, and I will give thee rest" (Exodus 33:14). That meant protection, provision, guidance, no fear, but perfect peace, in doing the will of God.

And as for Peter, the first preacher to the Jews and to the Gentiles, he was arrested with the apostles, put in prison, criticized, and forbidden by the authorities to preach the doctrine (Acts 5:27, 28). He answered, "We ought to obey God rather than men" and preached Jesus to the men on the council.

Peter and the other apostles were beaten (Acts 5:40), were told not to speak in the name of Jesus, and then let go. They departed, "rejoicing that they were counted worthy to suffer shame for his name" (verse 41), and "daily in the temple, and in every house, they ceased not to teach and preach Jesus Christ" (verse 42). Here was boldness instead of fear—doing what Christ had called them to do, counting on His promise "Lo, I am with you alway."

We know that Jesus as a man perfectly did the will of God. The record we have of Jesus from the age of twelve to His ascension shows us that the Lord Jesus obeyed God in every circumstance.

As a son He was obedient to Joseph and Mary, keeping the fifth commandment, "Honor thy father and thy mother."

In the temple at Jerusalem the "doctors" were astonished at His understanding and answers as He sat hearing them and asking questions. From His studies in the Scriptures at the synagogue in Nazareth, He showed a phenomenal memory and a brilliant mind, yet He was willing to return to Nazareth and be subject unto Joseph and Mary.

At His baptism Jesus did God's will in fulfilling all righteousness (Matthew 3:15).

In His ministry of teaching, preaching, healing, and doing all sorts of miracles, Jesus went through many difficult and strange circumstances. He fulfilled prophecy, taught God's truth and obeyed it, was criticized and misunderstood. He was hated, was deserted by His disciples, suffered, was rejected, and was crucified in doing God's will. He died and rose again from the dead in obedience to God's commandment (John 10:18). Because He was a perfect and obedient Son, God received Him in heaven, crowned Him with glory and honor, and seated Him on the throne at His right hand.

No other human being has gone through such happenings without failing somewhere along the line.

Jesus knew how to die to self in order to bring forth "much fruit" (John 12:24) and how to hate His life in order to keep it "unto life eternal" (John 12:25).

Jesus was not afraid of people or of circumstances. He always did and said the right thing because He was constantly in touch with God and depended on the Holy Spirit to lead Him.

Every Christian, regardless of his or her walk through life, will need to go through all sorts of difficulties and circumstances, pleasant and unpleasant, to be able to find out that there is only one Person, a real man, who never failed God, who will never fail us. "Jesus never fails."

The Old Testament is full of examples or illustrations of failure and success. Paul states in I Corinthians 10:11, "Now all these things happened unto them for ensamples: and they are written for our admonition [that we might learn from them and not make the same mistakes]." Then Paul goes on in verse 12: "Wherefore let him that thinketh he standeth take heed lest he fall."

The result of a Christian's failing to do God's will has been expressed this way: "However apparently good and lofty the pretext may be which induces us to disobey God's known will, it will be followed by an endless chain of sorrowful and disappointing circumstances."

One result of doing God's will is wonderful peace.

> What a treasure I have in this wonderful peace,
> Buried deep in the heart of my soul;
> So secure that no power can mine it away,
> While the years of eternity roll.
> Peace, peace, wonderful peace,
> Coming down from the Father above;
> Sweep over my spirit, forever, I pray,
> In fathomless billows of love.

One of the hardest things to accept is the death of a loved one.

A letter from a lady whose husband died suddenly, said this: "Always I've asked the Lord to take him first, and let me have the loneliness, for 'Dr. L' always had a dread of being alone. So the dear Lord did abundantly above—as He always does. He took him suddenly, quickly and without pain. What more could I possibly ask? Only when I, like Peter, look down at the waves (self-pity) do the tears flow. But it is not often, for I have so much joy from our forty-three years together. I am reminded, 'Joy is given; sorrow is only lent.' "

From another recently widowed Christian came these words: "Your letter came a few weeks ago, and it brought comfort to my heart. My husband's death was such a shock to us all—he went so suddenly. We had been married almost sixty years, and I can never remember his being away at Christmas time. This is hard, but I told my family we would all try to make someone else happy, and this would bring some joy to us. I find peace as I think of some hymns as 'What a Friend We Have in Jesus,' 'Until Then,' and 'I'll Never Leave Thee Lonely.' I know some day my heart will be healed and when God heals there will be no scar." Here are examples of II Corinthians 6:10: "As sorrowful, yet alway rejoicing."

A young couple preparing to go the mission field lost their first child. She was not normal, lived only about two years, and was taken suddenly to be with Jesus. The parents grieved, but got the victory over self, and praised God for their little one and the other children they hoped to have.

> Dead? She is breathless with wonder
> Understanding at last His grace,
> Feasting her eyes on the matchless
> Loveliness of His face.
> Dead? Can we call it dying,
> That life that is filled to the brim?
> Dead? In the light of His presence
> She is living forever with Him.

Accidents are things that often happen in the lives of Christians.

A young man who is very active in teen-work in a city torn by strife was riding to his headquarters on his motorcycle, a gift from a friend. His young son was up behind him. Suddenly a car sideswiped them; the accident resulted in the loss of a leg for the father and a long hospitalization for both father and son.

The shocking news traveled to Christian friends in many places. Immediately, those friends went faithfully and continually to the Throne of Grace to ask for that help promised to those in need (Hebrews 4:16).

Co-workers and local friends kept the work going with the help of the faithful wife and mother. Excerpts from "B's" letter read: " 'R's' infinite patience encouraged us continually and her complete handling of the entire operation, including radio, moved things along during our absence. Friends, board members, staff, our agent, and local pastor—all joined to fill in the gaps.

"Paul challenges us in Romans 12:1, 2 on the basis of all

Christ's goodness to present our bodies to Him as a living sacrifice. To those who do is promised that they will have that good, and acceptable, and perfect, will of God. There is nothing better than perfection and so, as we drove to the hospital anticipating the removal of my leg, 'R' and I were able to rejoice that for reasons He knew, but which we could only anticipate, we were still experiencing 'the perfect will of God.' What a source of comfort it was to us to know that things were not out of His dear control but that all was in His hands.

"Over and over I have been able to share Christ's joy and perfect peace with those who have come into our rooms. The Lord has done miracles in some lives and we are profoundly grateful for His using us to His glory.

"The radio family has grown and many more have taken an interest through our difficulties. We as a staff have learned to love each other better and give more of our selves through our trials. God's blessing continues to increase and we cannot help but praise Him for it all. Many have anticipated the special needs created by my loss of a limb and temporary loss of hearing and balance, and to them we give thanks.

"God makes no mistakes and so as we look to the future, we anticipate an enlarged ministry and blessings undreamed of from His dear hand.

"We are determined to see greater victories than ever now, unto His glory and praise. (The new leg is working well and the Holy Spirit is working in lives with great power.)

"Friends not only prayed but sent cards and money gifts to take care of the tremendous expense."

From "B's" wife came this word: "God has in a wonderful way provided for our every need thus far and He who is so faithful will continue to do so. We thank you for your part in helping to ease the burden. The Lord has sustained and given added grace and strength as the labor and burdens have increased. Truly I can testify to His sustaining grace. He has indeed been to each one of us all that we have needed."

Sickness and operations are very much a part of circumstances these days.

A friend who was a working mother and very active in Christian work had an experience which she agrees to have me share in this chapter.

In October, 1968, she noticed a swelling under her chin but thought it was no more than a swollen gland. In January, 1969, she had a few sharp pains in the left side of her neck when she swallowed; so decided to have it checked. The result was a diagnosis of cancer and an immediate operation. During the check-up period when she was sure she had cancer, she had such peace and calm from the Lord that the doctor noticed it and mentioned to her that he was surprised at her peace. She asked him if he knew Isaiah 26:3, and he said, "No, what is it?" Then she quoted the verse: "Thou wilt keep him in perfect peace, whose mind is stayed on thee: because he trusteth in thee." Then she said, "My mind is on the Lord," to which he replied, "That's wonderful."

The operation was scheduled for the following Monday.

The three children (young people) all came home Friday afternoon and a family discussion was held. Their mother told them she believed the cancer was in her body to glorify the Lord. They discussed healing without an operation, if the Lord chose to heal that way. As a family they prayed together, sang hymns of faith and praise for forty-five minutes, and had a wonderful time of Christian fellowship.

Word went out to praying friends in all directions, and the operation was started by putting radium needles in her tongue. In spite of a swollen tongue and discomfort, she had a good night's sleep. The reactions to this treatment were so unusual that the doctor said he could not operate on the next Friday. He said, "You know your case baffles me." She said, "I have Someone interceding for me." He just smiled.

The operation was re-scheduled for Wednesday and was due to last about five hours. Mrs. S. was moved to a two-bed ward with a lady, and they talked mostly about the Lord and trust and faith. A quotation from her letter reads: "Most of the time I was in a state of prayer and communion as I have never experienced before, and every day I expected the miracle of healing to happen."

When the anesthesiologist came on Tuesday afternoon late and told Mrs. S. that she was going to put her to sleep, she told her a little about the operation. Then she knew God was going to work His will and plan through an operation, rather than heal her immediately. "All right, Lord, whatever you want," she said. "Pour yourself into my body and take care of me.'"

The doctors removed all her lower teeth but three, all the floor of her mouth and quite a bit of her chin bone. When she came to on Friday she had a nose tube, neck tubes, a tracheotomy for breathing, a vaporizer hung around her neck, and intravenous feeding.

If spite of the discomfort she had no pain and needed no shots when the nurse came to give them. After a remarkable few days of beginning to recover and the removal of all tubes, she was allowed to go home six days earlier than expected by the doctor.

The doctor brought six internes to see Mrs. S. the third day after the operation and said, "This is the most phlegmatic person I have ever known." She thought he was talking about the phlegm she was bothered with, but her husband said the doctor meant "peaceful." She wrote later, "I never had a moment of fright or nerves, because of the peace that passeth understanding, that the Lord gives to those who trust in Him when there is no natural reason for peace and calm."

In due time the doctor rebuilt the floor of her mouth, made new gums to cover the one-third of jaw and chin bone that was left, and did such a marvelous job of sewing her up that she did not look very different.

Now she is back at work on her job, singing in the church choir and teaching a Sunday school class.

Her testimony is, "I wanted a miracle of healing for His glory. He wanted me, broken and mended by Him, a vessel fit for His use.

"It was a mountaintop experience and the operation was almost incidental to this wonderful peace and calm and communion I experienced. I just want to tell everyone what He has done for me and how wonderful it is to have Him for my Lord."

> Loved with everlasting love,
> Led by grace that love to know;
> Spirit, breathing from above,
> Thou hast taught me it is so!
> Oh! this full and perfect peace!
> Oh! this transport all divine!
> In a love which cannot cease,
> I am His and He is mine.

The loss of things that mean much can come into the lives of all Christians.

A young couple working for the Lord in jungle camp near a river were tested this way. As a co-worker floated down the swift river to the men's swimming hole, he spotted the husband "D" on the river bank. He called out, "Hey, 'D,' your wife is upriver practicing rejoicing."

"Yeah, 'S' and I are learning to praise God in every circumstance," replied the young man.

"She just lost her contact lens in the river," called the friend as he floated by.

"She what?" gasped the young husband.

"She lost her contact, but she's praising the Lord, anyhow," the friend replied.

"She is? Well, praise the Lord!"

That was quite a loss and a test but the very next week "D" lost his wedding band in the same river, and it hardly daunted him. He simply praised the Lord and grew in Him. This was God's purpose that he might grow up into Christ in all things (Ephesians 4:15).

The first reaction a person has to a sudden, difficult, or unusual circumstance is fear. We all hate changes or interruptions in our usual lives.

The "fear not's" of the New Testament are encouraging. Here are some of them:

God's Providences

In the Supernatural

1. Luke 2:9-11, Angels to shepherds, "Fear not," be joyful, your Savior is born (Good news).
2. Mark 5:36, Jesus to Jairus, "Be not afraid, only believe" (in a miracle).
3. Matthew 14:24-34, Jesus, walking on the sea to his disciples, "It is I; be not afraid" (His presence with them).
4. Matthew 17:5-7, The transfigured Jesus to the three disciples, "Arise and be not afraid" (of God's voice).
5. Mark 16:8 and Matthew 28:5, 6, Angel to women at empty tomb, "Fear not . . . ye seek Jesus . . . . He is risen" (God's power over death).

131

1. There were those men who feared the people: the Jewish and Roman politicians; the parents of the man born blind, who feared the Jews who would put them out of the synagogue; and the captain of the officers of the temple, who feared being stoned by the people who liked the apostles because of their healing and teaching. (Acts 5:26).

2. In Matthew 10:26 Jesus said to His disciples, warning of persecutors, "Fear them not" and in verse 28, "Fear not them which kill the body . . . but fear him which is able to destroy both soul and body in hell."

3. In Luke 12:32 Jesus said, "Fear not, little flock, for it is your Father's good pleasure to give you the kingdom."

4. Christ knew fear. We are told in Hebrews 5:7: "He had offered up prayers and supplications with strong crying and tears unto him that was able to save him from death, and was heard in that he feared."

   As a man Jesus shrank from the awful agony, suffering, and shame of the cross and all it meant. He received strength through prayer to go through it triumphantly when He said, "Not my will, but thine be done."

   He had come to do God's will (Hebrews 10:7), to give His body as the only sacrifice that would please God (verses 6, 8).

   "Though he were a Son, yet learned he obedience by the things which he suffered and . . . became the author of eternal salvation unto all that obey him" (Hebrews 5:8, 9). Without this work of His there would be no "kingdom" for His disciples or us.

   Therefore we can say, "The Lord is my helper and I will not fear what man shall do unto me" (Hebrews 13:6).

   Before He went to the cross Jesus said these wonderful words: "Peace I leave with you, my peace I give unto you . . . . Let not your heart be troubled, neither let it be afraid" (John 14:27).

5. To Paul in danger at Corinth the same Lord said, "Be not afraid, but speak . . . For I am with thee and no man shall . . . hurt thee" (Acts 18:9, 10).

132

Again in danger of shipwreck after fasting and prayer, the Lord's angel said, "Fear not, Paul, thou must be brought before Ceasar [in Rome where he longed to go]" (Acts 27:24).

And Paul said in II Corinthians 7:5, 6: " . . . our flesh had no rest, but we were troubled on every side: without were fightings, within were fears. Nevertheless God . . . comforted us by the coming of Titus."

So Paul could write in Philippians 4:6, 7: "Be careful [or full of care] for nothing [no event] but in every thing [every event] by prayer and supplication with thanksgiving let your requests be made known unto God. And the peace of God, which passeth all understanding, shall keep your hearts and minds through Christ Jesus."

What is the cross for us? It is the struggles we have as we do the will of God. "Thy will be done" does not mean resignation but cooperation.

The problem is how to know the will of God.

1. There must be willingness to do it.
2. There must be much prayer for guidance.
3. There should be a message from the Bible.
4. There are usually circumstances to be considered.
5. There must be yieldedness to God's plan. Then the result will be light in our minds and peace in our hearts.

In the matter of marriage for Christians, circumstances and prayer must play a large part in deciding the will of God.

A man and woman, very active in Christian work, fell in love with each other. They were the same age and seemed suitable for each other in every way. The question was whether it was the will of God for them to marry. Circumstances were against them, but they hoped the Lord would make the necessary changes. After much prayer, waiting, struggling with self, real heartache and agony, the answer came, "No." Acceptance of God's will brought peace and eventual happiness to each in doing the work of God through separate lives of fruitful and interesting service, rather than being together in misery out of God's will.

A young Christian engineer in his late twenties thought he had found the right girl to be his wife. He believed this to be the will of God because of unusual circumstances. It was a shock when she did not agree with him and turned him down. The blow was so hard that he took a long trip with a Christian man to see a mission field. God showed the young man that His will for him was to go into the ministry.

He obeyed the Lord, gave up his engineering, went to seminary, found the right wife, and became a successful minister.

How wonderful it is when the Lord brings together two dedicated Christians and leads them, as a team, into a life of successful service for Him!

A businessman in his thirties had not met the right girl and thought he would probably remain a bachelor. He went south in the early spring to lose a cold that had hung on and, because of his interest in the Lord's work, he went to a mission that was being conducted for sailors on Saturday nights.

At the piano was a vivacious young lady in her early thirties, who had decided she would probably never marry because she knew no suitable men who loved her Lord as she did.

They were attracted immediately to each other through their love for the Bible, the hope of the imminent return of Christ for His own, Christian hymns (she played and he sang), and their concern for the lost. After much prayer to know the will of God, for there would be difficult adjustments ahead, they were married and lived devotedly as husband and wife and parents for many years, faithfully serving the Lord together. (I know because I am their daughter.)

Sometimes through circumstances God changes our plans. In the fall of 1970 a friend and I were staying in a motel in Asheville, North Carolina, for the weekend.

On Sunday morning the weather was bad for my allergies; so we decided to go to church by television. This was definitely God's plan, for we turned to a channel where a delightful service was being televised. The minister of the church soon announced that he wanted one of the members to come forward to give her testimony.

A most attractive, beautifully dressed and enthusiastic young girl walked up on the platform and stood before the microphone. She was "Miss South Carolina," the runner-up for the Miss America title the previous week.

She thanked the members of the congregation who had prayed for her and those who had met her at the airport when she returned from Atlantic City.

Some of her friends had told her they lost ten years of their lives when she did not win the crown, but she felt from the start of her decision to enter the contest that this was God's will for her, whatever the outcome. Some of the church members wanted to know what she and Miss Texas talked about as they sat together waiting to hear who would be called next as the runner-up. She told them that she said to "Miss Texas," whom she had met but did not really know, "I feel that however this turns out it will be according to the will of God." Quickly, Miss Texas replied, "I feel the same way." "Are you a believer too?" asked Miss South Carolina. "Oh, yes!" was the reply. Just then the call came for Miss South Carolina to come forward as the runner-up. She was sure God's will had been done and was genuinely happy that another Christian had won the crown. So, to the church audience and to all of us watching by TV, she joyously said, "I don't feel that I lost; I feel that I came back a winner."

It is not what happens to us that counts; it is how we take it!

Prayer is a very important part of our lives as Christians.

A missionary in the Philippines was very successful in translating the Scriptures into the language of the Balango tribe. Through hearing the Good News read to them by the missionary, many of the tribe's people, including five witch doctors, were saved. They continued to love hearing the Word of God but could not see any need of praying to Him. "J," the missionary, wondered how God would answer her prayers to teach these Christians to pray. Most unexpectedly the answer came, through shocking circumstances. "J" was riding in a helicopter, seated on five tons of bags of cement being carried to a town for building purposes. As the copter descended for a landing the Balango people, who were watching, saw it suddenly crash. When the dust cleared enough to see, the people rushed in to rescue their missionary friend. Frantically, they dug into the pile of cement bags until they uncovered her, still alive, but hurt, and carried her to a house nearby.

She had a broken clavicle, three broken ribs, and a partly collapsed lung. All the first night the nationals worried over her and the Christians all prayed! How thankful "J" was for this circumstance that God used in order that her prayers might be answered.

The president of a bank wrote to a friend, "For more than a year I have been totally blind. I am not praying for restoration of sight—but I am praying with Paul for grace and strength which I am thankful to say He has given me." "Trouble?" we say. Nothing else probably could have made him fix his unseeing eyes on spiritual things so hard and earnestly that now he actually pities the man who has good eyes but does not know the Lord.

> Fear not, little flock, whatever your lot,
> He enters all rooms, "the doors being shut":
> He never forsakes, He never is gone,
> So count on His presence, in darkness and dawn[4]

In discussing today's complicated living with me, a Christian neighbor mentioned the difficulties of "people in our circumstances," who work themselves almost to death to make a living and rear a family. Her problems were business, property, finances, and dealing with other people.

An old lady was asked what she would do now that her husband had died and she would have to make her way alone in the world. "You're going to have a hard time, Granny, under the circumstances." "Yes," the dear old lady replied, "under my circumstances, I would have a hard time. But, don't you know, Honey, God doesn't want His children to live *under* the circumstances? I'm living *over* them—*above* them!"

C. H. McIntosh has written, "We never can know what is in our hearts until circumstances arise to draw it out. Peter did not imagine that he could deny his Lord; but when he got into circumstances which were calculated to act upon his peculiar weakness, he showed that the weakness was there." Jesus "knew all men, And needed not that any should testify of man, for He knew what was in man" (John 2:24, 25).

"How can you look so pleasant tonight?" a man asked his friend. "You have had a score of interruptions this afternoon, and you hoped to do a lot of work." "That's all right," he answered. "Every morning I give my day to Christ; then I take what He sends. These interruptions come in the way of duty. Why should I complain about the service He has appointed?" This man's secret

136

is to be found in Colossians 3:1, 2: " . . . seek those things which are above . . . . Set your affection on things above."

Sometimes the answer to prayer is delayed, as it was for Moses. The answer to his prayer to enter the promised land was kept back for centuries till he stood there with Jesus Himself. Elijah's prayer to die because of his "trying" circumstances was refused; for the glory of the fiery chariot and the whirlwind were waiting for him, and God had still more for Elijah to do before He took him to heaven.

The writing of this book is a testimony to God's leading through delays, stops, starts, and many most unusual and trying circumstances.

After writing my first book, *God's Timing in the Kentucky Mountains*, which seemed to be everybody's book, the thought came to me, "I would like to write a book that could be just the Lord's and mine."

One of my great disappointments in life has been the failure in Christians (and that included me) to act Christlike. I decided to search the New Testament to see how Christians should behave. The result is this book.

It could not be written until I could free myself from certain responsibilities, such as a large unneeded home and Christian activities which others could take over, and could take a much-needed writing course.

In January, 1965, I was working away on the lessons of the writing course and making enough progress to believe I could start work on this book. I had not felt so well in many years and was thoroughly enjoying myself.

A spider or some insect bit me on my shin as I walked around in the back yard of my Florida home. A hard scab formed with fluid underneath, and pressure on a small vein caused my legs to swell and ache. This was the beginning of troubles. I was given a wrong diagnosis and several wrong treatments; infection set in, and my system became so weakened that I developed many new allergies that are peculiar to Florida.

With great effort I struggled on with the writing course and started looking up verses in the New Testament for the chapters in the book.

By July I was so miserable with aches, pains, nervousness, and sleeplessness that I went to a hospital near Harlan, Kentucky, to

137

be x-rayed for what I thought might be an ulcer. Alone in my private room I decided that a good way to spend sleepless hours was to look up Bible verses.

Seven chapters had been covered, and it was now time to work on the eighth, "Circumstances." This chapter actually began on a hospital bed late at night as I enjoyed several hours with my Bible, my pen, and a pad looking for suitable verses.

X-rays showed no ulcer; but before many weeks went by I landed in a hospital in Philadelphia, Pennsylvania, for more x-rays and allergy tests to learn the cause of my increasing discomfort and sleeplessness.

The result was I had gallstones, colitis, and severe allergies to foods, dust, and, of all things, cotton. (Cotton was the cause of my sleeplessness.)

I was too weak for an operation; so I was put on a strict diet with proper medication and waited in the hospital to have my nose desensitized to cotton, so that I could live in a world that seemed to me to be full of it.

Instead of staying a short while, I was there for five weeks, getting weaker and becoming allergic to other things and, worst of all, to newsprint!

The Lord kept me there for His purpose to answer my prayers for a niece, who was wanting to be saved. In my room she met a Bible-teaching friend of mine who was visiting near my niece's home. That led to several discussions and contacts that brought my niece and her husband to Christ and into a very spiritual church.

When I told my allergist in Philadelphia and later on another one in Florida that I wanted to write this book, the Philadelphia doctor said he thought such a book was needed, but he did not see how I could possibly do it. The Florida doctor looked startled and said, "That'll be the day!"

I knew that God would make it possible for me to do what He had put in my heart. There were given perfect peace and sufficient grace to wait through all the delays for the needed strength to do the job. The writing course had to be dropped. I could not handle all that paper and ink.

Very slowly—in intervals of a few minutes, of a half hour or an hour, and sometimes of two hours—the research and writing have been done. For a person who likes to start things and finish them

138

quickly, this has been a time of testing, with learning new lessons of patience. Often I have been tempted to stop, but always there has been the pressure of the Holy Spirit to keep me going. I know now that I was not ready six years ago to write this book. There has been a reason for every start and stop, and I have learned very much more of God's grace.

In the hospital in Philadelphia I thought perhaps the Lord was through with me down here and would take me home to heaven. It seemed to me there would never be a more convenient time; but as I read Philippians 1:20-25, I began to wonder.

I felt very close to my Lord in the hospital; and as the words Paul had written poured out at me from the page, I turned my heart to the Lord Jesus and asked: "Is this word for me? Am I to stay here longer? Is there something more for me to do? Can I become strong enough to do Thy work and Thy will in the days ahead?" Assurance came that this was so. I knew I would need to cooperate with the Lord and with the doctor if I was to get well.

Through the help of the Lord and the doctors, my health has been restored except for inconvenient allergies to fabrics and newsprint.

Eight chapters have been written now, and two more are ahead, God willing. In His time and way God's will is being done and I praise Him!

Right here I would like to suggest seven results of doing God's will:

1. Philippians 1:12—The gospel is furthered.
2. Romans 8:28—We become more conformed to the image (likeness) of Christ.
3. John 12:24, 25—We produce much spiritual fruit unto life eternal.
4. II Corinthians 7:4—We learn to be joyful in all tribulation.
5. II Corinthians 4:8, 9, 10—We know freedom from distress, perplexity, despair, loneliness, and being cast down in order that the life of Christ in us may be seen.
6. Acts 5:41—When persecuted for Christ's sake, we can be like the disciples, who rejoiced that they were counted worthy to suffer shame for Jesus' name.
7. II Corinthians 4:17, 18—We can look beyond the circumstances to the glorious, eternal results.

What better way can I close this chapter than with these words from the hymn "How Firm a Foundation":

"Fear not, I am with thee, O be not dismayed,
   For I am thy God, I will still give thee aid.
   I'll strengthen thee, help thee, and cause thee to stand,
   Upheld by My gracious, omnipotent hand.

"When through fiery trials thy pathway shall lie,
   My grace, all sufficient, shall be thy supply;
   The flames shall not hurt thee, I only design
   Thy dross to consume and thy gold to refine."

CHAPTER NINE

Toward

Opposition—God's Testing

We sing "Onward, Christian soldiers, Marching as to war"; "Stand up, stand up for Jesus, Ye soldiers of the cross"; "Sound the battle cry! See, the foe is nigh"; and other hymns that include words such as "army," "armor," "shield and banner," "war," "gates of hell," "conflict," and "strife."

Why do we as Christians sing these warlike hymns? Who opposes us? Who is our enemy, our dangerous foe? He is none other than Satan, called in Revelation 12:7-10 "the dragon," "that old serpent," "the Devil," and "the accuser of our brethren."

Because we have such a foe we should find out all we can about him. We should know whom we are up against and what the Bible tells us of his opposition to God and God's servants. We should know how to act toward him.

To "oppose" is "to resist, set against, contend with in speech or action, to show hostility, to be contrary on opposing sides, to defy, dispute, be antagonistic; to be an enemy, a rebel, a foe—to withstand or contradict."

Satan qualifies for every one of these definitions. He is against God and God's people, accusing us "before our God day and night" (Revelation 12:10). He is a mighty, dangerous, fierce enemy to deal with.

He appeared in Genesis 3:1 as the subtle serpent who tempted and tricked Eve—a crafty, wily, sly creature. Through Adam's folly in listening to Eve and disobeying God, the whole human race came under Satan's power.

Where did Satan come from? In Isaiah 14:12 he is called "Lucifer, son of the morning," who, in verses 13 and 14, said in

141

his heart, "*I will* ascend into heaven, *I will* exalt my throne above the stars of God; *I will* sit also upon the mount of the congregation, in the sides of the north, *I will* ascend above the heights of the clouds; *I will* be like the Most High."

In Ezekiel 28:12-15 there is one who is called "the anointed cherub that covereth." Many Bible scholars believe this is none other than Satan, a being created to be God's minister, one who in verse 12 is described as "full of wisdom, and perfect in beauty." In verse 13 he is spoken of as having been "in Eden, the garden of God"; and in verse 14 we are told that he was "upon the holy mountain of God." Then we read in verse 15: "Thou wast perfect in thy ways from the day thou wast created, till iniquity was found in thee." And what was that iniquity? The answer is in the first nine words of verse 17: "Thine heart was lifted up because of thy beauty." This reveals the pride of Satan in the five "I will's" of Isaiah 14. Here was a most beautiful angel who, because of pride and beauty and position, wanted to take God's place of power and be like Him. As a result, Satan was cast out of heaven with his angels who followed him (Revelation 12:9) and will some day be in that place of "everlasting fire, prepared for the devil and his angels" (Matthew 25:41).

The Pharisees in Matthew 9:34 mentioned devils (demons) and the prince of the devils as being powerful. Again in Matthew 12:24 they called Satan Beelzebub, the prince of the devils. In Revelation 12:3, 4 we are told that one third of the stars of heaven (angels) were drawn to the "great red dragon." We see then that Satan caused one third of the angels in heaven to follow him in disobedience to God; and in Revelation 12:9 the great dragon and his angels are identified with Satan, the deceiver of the whole world, who was cast into the earth.

God created angels to be ministering spirits (Hebrews 1:7) to worship Him (Hebrews 1:6). When Jesus commanded the demons to come out of the man of Gadara (Matthew 8:28-32) and go into the swine, these demons were some of Satan's "ministers" who recognized Jesus as the Son of God (verse 29) and knew He would some day condemn and torment them at the time of judgment. In James 2:19 we read, "The devils [demons] also believe, and tremble."

God created man to obey Him and to have unbroken fellowship with Him. Satan spoiled all that. Satan wanted, and still wants, to control men and nations in order to weaken and destroy them (Isaiah 14:12) in hell. God wants to strengthen men and nations by their obeying Him on earth and in heaven (Revelation 21:24, 26).

In Daniel, chapter 10, after Daniel had prayed and fasted twenty-one days for his nation Israel, a Man appeared.

The description of this Man (Daniel 10:5, 6) is similar to that of the glorified Christ, whom John saw in Revelation 1:12-16. Many Bible scholars consider this man to be the Lord. This Man spoke to Daniel, saying he had been sent to Daniel to answer his prayers of these three weeks (Daniel 10:2). These prayers had been heard (verse 12), but He had been hindered from coming by the Prince of the kingdom of Persia, one and twenty days (verse 13). "Michael, one of the chief princes [an archangel], came to help me," said the Man.

This Man came to tell Daniel what the future held for his nation, Israel (verse 14), which was in captivity under the Persian king Cyrus, a mighty ruler over the nation in that day.

This Man (the Lord) told Daniel in verse 20, "[I will] return to fight with the prince of Persia [a heathen king ruled by Satan]" to defeat him, "and when I am gone forth, lo, the prince of Grecia shall come [another heathen king ruling under Satan's power]." "But," said the Man in verse 21, "I will shew thee that which is noted in the scripture of truth; and there is none that holdeth with me in these things, but Michael your prince." Here we have Scriptural truth that Satan wants to rule the nations through powerful kings. Only Michael, a powerful, obedient angel of God, could stand with the Lord in opposition to Satanic powers of evil and overcome them.

Who is Michael? In Daniel 12:1 he is "the great prince which standeth for the children of thy people [Israel]." in Jude 9 he is the archangel who contended with the devil and could not accuse him, but said, "The Lord rebuke thee." In Revelation 12:7 "there was war in heaven; Michael and his angels fought against the dragon, and the dragon fought and his angels." The winner is Michael with his angels.

It is evident in what I have just written and from Zechariah 3:2 that only one person can win over Satan: "The Lord rebuke thee, O Satan; even the Lord that hath chosen Jerusalem rebuke thee." Here we have God's refusing to allow Satan to have permanent control over a city which is one day to be the capital of the world. "At that time they shall call Jerusalem the throne of the Lord; and all the nations shall be gathered unto it, to the name of the Lord, to Jerusalem; neither shall they walk any more after the imagination of their evil heart" (Jeremiah 3:17).

So we see Satan wanting to control cities as well as nations and people.

One day he is going to completely fill and control a world ruler—that "man of sin [lawlessness]," "the son of perdition [damnation]" (II Thessalonians 2:3). He will oppose God, exalt himself to be worshiped as God (verse 4); but his reign will be short and brought to a sudden end when, in verse 8, "the Lord shall consume [him] with the spirit of his mouth, and shall destroy [him] with the brightness of His coming."

Satan tempted (tested) Eve; she succumbed.

Satan tried his wiles on Job and failed. We learn from the story of Job that God allows Satan to tempt or test a believer, but to go only so far and no further.

We learn that Satan can appear in heaven (Job 1:6) as well as to go "to and fro" in the earth and walk "up and down in it" (verse 7). Satan knew all about Job—his excellent character, his fear of God and accompanying behavior (verse 8). We read that Satan was permitted to test Job's motives (verses 9-12) by taking all he possessed (including his children) away from him, but not to put his hand on Job.

Job did not fail God in this test, although he was shocked and grieved, for he "fell down upon the ground and worshiped," and said, " . . . the Lord gave, and the Lord hath taken away; blessed be the name of the Lord (verses 20, 21). "In all this Job sinned not, nor charged God foolishly" (verse 22). (I wonder how we would have acted?)

Satan did not give up! He does not accept defeat easily! So he appeared before the Lord in heaven and asked permission to try again—this time to ask God to touch Job's body to see whether he would not curse God (Job 2:4, 5). Again God limited Satan's power by allowing him to cover Job's body with sore boils, but not to take his life (verse 6). The affliction of the boils caused Job's wife to suggest that he "curse God, and die." But Job accepted this further test and trial as coming from God (verse 10) and did not "sin with his lips." (He did not complain! Would we?)

Days went by. "Comforters" came in the form of four friends who neither understood nor could help him in his distress. Job knew " . . . the arrows of the Almighty . . . the terrors of God" were causing his trouble (Job 6:4), and in verses 8-9 he prayed for death. That request was not granted, for God had a wonderful future for Job.

Job's faith in God never faltered, for in chapter 13:15 he exclaimed, "Though he slay me, yet will I trust in him; but I will maintain mine own ways before him." Here was Job's unrecognized problem, as we will see later: "I will maintain mine own ways before him."

Job believed in a personal redeemer from sin and in the resurrection of the body. In chapter 19:25-27, Job stated his faith and his certainty of life after death: " . . . I know that my redeemer liveth . . . and though after my skin worms destroy this body, yet in my flesh shall I see God: Whom I shall see for myself . . . . " (This was written centuries before Christ came.)

In Job 23:3 he exclaimed, "Oh that I knew where I might find him! that I might come even to his seat!" Job in his misery could not reach the presence of God, but in verse 10 Job knew enough of God's grace to say, "But he knoweth the way that I take: when he hath tried me, I shall come forth as gold." In verse 14 he trusted God for the purpose in this testing, though Job did not yet know what that was: "For he performeth the thing that is appointed for me."

In chapter 27:4 when his "comforters" tried to make him admit to some sin in his life, Job said, "My lips shall not speak wickedness, nor my tongue utter deceit." He would not confess a sin he did not feel guilty of.

Then God, in chapters 38 and 39, spoke to Job out of a whirlwind, telling of His mighty power in creation and answering Job's request in chapter 23:3 that he might find God.

As a result Job sees himself in chapter 40:4 as "vile"; he is no longer self-righteous (maintaining his "own ways" before God). Then in Job 42:5 Job has his vision open to see God as He is: is: " . . . now mine eye seeth thee. Wherefore [because of God's holiness and power] I abhor myself, and repent in dust and ashes."

The result of all this suffering and trial was that "the Lord turned the captivity of Job, when he prayed for his friends." God had told Job's friends (chapter 42:7, 8) they had spoken wrongly to Job. For that they must offer a burnt offering for themselves (in confession of sin). When they did that (verses 8 and 9) Job would pray for them, "for him will I accept." As they "did according as the Lord commanded them: the Lord also accepted Job." Job received from the Lord "twice as much as he had before." After all this testing the Bible tells us, "So the Lord blessed the latter end of Job more than his beginning . . . " (Job 42:12) because the testing by Satan proved him to be indeed a God-fearing man.

We can learn many lessons from this account of Job: his suffering and trials coming from the permissive hand of a loving God for Job's good.

Here we see a servant of God being tested from above and from below as Satan is permitted to try his limited power over a man who did not fail his God.

When I was growing up, my father was the vice president and general manager of Lukens Steel Company in Coatesville, Pennsylvania. He was intensely interested in the quality of steel the plate mills produced.

I was always delighted when Father asked me to go with him to the plant to see any part of the steel-making process.

What especially fascinated me was watching the pouring of steel. Red hot, fiery, boiling steel, with sparks flying in all directions, was being poured from a furnace into a huge ladle and then from the ladle into sets of ingot-molds placed below.

As soon as this exciting "show" was over, Father and I went to another building, where ingots were reheated in special furnaces. When an ingot reached the right temperature, it was lifted by machinery out of the furnace and moved by an overhead crane to a rolling mill. There I would stand by my father as we watched that thick, fiery-red steel ingot being passed back and forth between the huge rolls. Water was sprayed and salt spread on the surface of the rapidly forming steel plate to take off the scales.

When the plate had been rolled to the right thickness, width, and length, it had lost its intense heat and color. It was then ready for testing to see whether it would meet the specifications of a special order from a purchaser.

Nothing pleased my father more than to go later to the testing department in the plant and to find that the steel from that plate met the required standards. We watched as a small piece of steel, cut from the plate, was placed upright in a special machine with the ends securely clamped above and below. The machinery was started, slowly pulling the square of steel from above and below, stretching it to its breaking point in order to test its tensile strength.

I can see myself, a little girl, standing with my father in front of that testing machine watching to see how long that small piece of steel could take that steady, heavy, constant pulling before breaking in the center. If the break came too soon, that specially prepared plate of steel could not be marketed; it would have failed to meet the requirements. It could not be used.

Suppose an enemy of the steel company had slipped up, and, unobserved, thrown in some destructive chemical as the steel was being prepared; the result, an unusable product.

As Father and I would continue watching, we would hear a sharp noise and see the piece of steel break in two. The test was over. Immediately the workers (and Father also) would check to see at what point the piece had broken.

What gratification it was to my father and to the workmen and what excitement for me when the steel proved to have the tensile strength necessary to meet the commercially required standards. The plate could be sold and used with safety.

One summer when I was fifteen, our family went on a trip to Alaska and the western part of the United States. The only way to cross the continent in those days was by a train drawn by steam engines. On the return trip I remember the train stopping at a small station to take on water for the long pull ahead. There was plenty of time for Father and me to walk past the long train of passenger cars to see the engines. He wanted to be sure the boilers of those engines were capable of pulling that heavy train, full of people, across the hot desert and over the high mountains. When we reached the two engines, Father looked for and found the name of the steelmaker on each engine. Then he smiled, turned to me, and said, "I'm not afraid those boilers will blow up under pressure; they're made of Lukens steel!"

We have an enemy, Satan, who wants to destroy us, to make us fail in our Christian lives and be unusable. But we also have a Man who "was in all points tempted [tested] like as we are yet without sin" (Hebrews 4:15).

A mighty fortress is our God,
A bulwark never failing;
Our helper He, amid the flood
Of mortal ills prevailing.
For still our ancient foe
Doth seek to work us woe;
His craft and power are great,
And armed with cruel hate,
On earth is not his equal.

Did we in our own strength confide,
Our striving would be losing,
Were not the right man on our side,
The Man of God's own choosing.
Dost ask who that may be?
Christ Jesus, it is He;
Lord Sabaoth His name,
From age to age the same,
And He must win the battle.

Satan did his best to destroy this Man, Jesus Christ, from the time He was born until He cried from the cross, "It is finished." Herod tried to destroy Jesus by having the little boy children in Bethlehem killed. Satan tried to have Jesus cast Himself down to destruction, out of God's will, from the pinnacle of the temple. The people of Nazareth tried to throw Him over a cliff to destroy Him (Luke 4:28, 29). The Jews tried to kill Him by stoning (John 8:59); the Pharisees planned to destroy Him (Matthew 12: 14); His enemies, the Jewish leaders, plotted His death (Matthew 26:3 and 4); Satan entered into Judas Iscariot (Luke 22:3) to sell Jesus that He might be killed; the multitudes said to release Barabbas and destroy Jesus; and Satan, whose weapon is death, thought he really was accomplishing his purpose when he got Jesus on a cross.

Satan's wages is death, the final payment or reward he gives to those who follow him.

Satan's object is to weaken and destroy. God's purpose and desire is to save and strengthen.

Twice in the New Testament we have the phrase "the power of darkness." It was used by Jesus in Luke 22:53 when He said to the chief priests, captains of the temple, and Jewish elders who came to arrest Him, " . . . this is your hour and the power of darkness." Paul in Colossians 1:13 tells us that God "hath delivered us from the power of darkness, and hath translated us into the kingdom of His dear Son."

Satan's kingdom is powerful darkness; Christ's kingdom is glorious light. Satan's destiny is hell; Jesus calls him in John 17:12 "the son of perdition." "Perdition" is "the loss of the soul or hope of salvation." God loved us enough and Jesus loved us enough to die so that "through death he might destroy him that had the power of death, that is, the devil" (Hebrews 2:14). For the Christian there is the wonderful fact that we no longer are in Satan's kingdom, but have been taken into God's kingdom through faith in Christ's work for us on the cross.

In order to do this for mankind, Jesus Christ, as a man, had to stand the test to meet God's standards and win the victory over Satan.

In what ways are we tempted? The answer is in I John 2:16, the three ways being "the lust of the flesh, and the lust of the eyes, and the pride of life." "Lust" means "intense desire."

The first human being to be tempted (tested) was Eve in the garden of Eden. She failed in each one of the three testings. Satan usually strikes first at our eyes. Eve in Genesis 3:6 made the mistake of going to the tree and looking at it. The tree looked good for fruit (lust of the flesh); it was pleasant to the eyes (lust of the eyes), and it would make one wise (pride of life). She yielded to temptation by taking some fruit and eating it. The result was not what she hoped for when she gave the fruit to Adam and he, the head of the human race, disobeyed God by eating it.

Satan, a deceiver and a liar, is always promising something he cannot fulfill. What Adam and Eve received was death, rather than life; evil, rather than good; shame, rather than pride; and, worst of all, loss of fellowship with a God of love.

Where Eve lost, Jesus Christ won.

After His baptism Jesus was "led up of the spirit into the wilderness to be tempted of the devil" (Matthew 4:1). He was tempted (verse 3) to satisfy His hunger (lust of the flesh) by commanding that the stones be made bread; he was tempted (verse 6) to cast Himself down from the pinnacle of the temple so that he could be rescued by angels (pride of life); he was tempted (verse 8) to fall down and worship Satan in order to receive all the kingdoms of the world and their glory (lust of the eyes).

How did Jesus respond to these suggestions and offers? By quoting passages of Scripture from the Old Testament—Deuteronomy 8:3, 6:16, and 6:13.

You will notice that Satan always started with the word "If," trying to cause Jesus to doubt His deity. Satan was trying to cause Jesus to act out of the will of God, to go contrary to God's plan for His Son, finally revealing what he was really after: "fall down and worship me." Then Jesus ordered Satan away with the words "Thou shalt worship the Lord, thy God [Satan's creator], and him only shalt thou serve" (Matthew 4:10).

How did Jesus return from these days of severe testing? He did so, we are told, in Luke 4:14, "in the power of the Spirit." He came out stronger than when He went into that place of testing.

> Conquering now and still to conquer,
> Rideth a King in His might,
> Leading the host of all the faithful
> Into the midst of the fight.

Jesus was well acquainted with Satan. He said about him: "The prince of this world [shall] be cast out" (John 12:31), "the prince of this world cometh, and hath nothing in me [could not get inside Jesus]" (John 14:30); and "the prince of this world is judged." This judgment happened at the cross (John 12:31-33).

Paul was well acquainted with Satan. He called him in Ephesians 2:2 "the prince of the power of the air, the spirit that now worketh in the children of disobedience." Notice that Satan is *now* in the children of disobedience and is *working* in them.

Jesus warned His disciples that they would go out as sheep in the midst of wolves (vicious creatures) and that they should beware of men (Satan's tools) who would hate and persecute them for His sake (Matthew 10:16-25). His disciples were to expect the same treatment He received. He asked them to "fear not them . . . but rather fear him which is able to destroy both soul and body in hell" (Matthew 10:28). There can be no friendship with Satan nor any compromise if believers are to win the battle.

What are some of Satan's tricks?

150

1. He can hinder men as he did the Lord for three weeks in Daniel, as he did Paul in Thessalonica (I Thessalonians 2:18) where Paul said, " . . . we would have come unto you . . . but Satan hindered us."

2. He can hinder the spreading of the Gospel. From Japan comes a letter asking prayer for a small church where the new pastor's behavior is preventing the Holy Spirit from working.

3. He can cause trying delays in the construction of a needed church in Japan.

4. He can work through accidents, illnesses, strange diseases on mission fields as expressed on a prayer card from India: "This effort to reach lost souls with the Gospel is not going unchallenged by the enemy of souls. Already he is raising many obstacles and much opposition, so that each member of the staff there is under attack in some way—accident, illness, etc." God's word tells us in II Timothy 3:11 that out of all the persecutions and afflictions that Paul endured the Lord delivered him.

5. Satan can cause all sorts of unusual problems in Christian work, such as in a ministry by boat on a river in Peru, where souls were being saved and local churches established in towns. The missionary learned to say, "No problem; there's a way through" and "When Satan attacks I claim the blood of Christ and go on."

6. Satan can bring believers into bondage, through sin, as expressed in a letter from a missionary in Columbia, S. A.: "We have a new crop of nine believers, all very weak and not acting much like Christians. They need a lot of care, encouragement, and patience. We desperately need prayer for those who are bound by Satan. Please pray for us. We are not called to defeat, but to victory."

7. Satan can try to stop any testimony for Christ through the written word—letters, magazines, or books—as he has been doing to me with this book. In the hospital in Philadelphia (see Chapter Eight on "Circumstances") in the early hours of my first day there, I had a severe attack from the Devil. Having had much opposition from him during my many years of Christian service, I was quick to recognize my opponent and his way of trying to get control of me in my lowest-ever physical condition and at the darkest hour of the morning. A verse of a hymn came to me, and later, verses from Psalm 27, which brought deliverance from Satan's power as I claimed victory over him through Christ. Later when the doctor's

tests proved that I had become allergic to newsprint, I said to myself, "There we go! Satan does not want me to write that book and is trying to stop me." By God's grace, Satan has not won, even though the writing of this chapter has been the hardest of all. The powers of darkness have been pressing hard, but, claiming victory through the blood of Christ, I have been able to continue.

8. Satan can transform himself into an angel of light (II Corinthians 11:13-15), using false apostles (teachers), deceitful workers, ministers of righteousness to deceive. He will do anything to make the Word of God of none effect.

9. Satan can walk about "as a roaring lion . . . seeking whom he may devour" (I Peter 5:8), wanting to frighten you and tear you apart. He seems to be doing this successfully today through the drug traffic in our country.

James writes: "Submit yourselves therefore to God. Resist the devil and he will flee from you" (chapter 4:7). "Submit" means "to yield to" and "resist" means to "stand firm against." This is just what James did and what a Christian must do.

What can we understand about this problem of evil and opposition?

"God cannot be tempted with evil, neither tempteth he any man" (James 1:13). God is the source of all good. Then where does temptation come from? In chapter 1, verse 14, James says, "But every man is tempted when he is drawn away of his own lust, and enticed." The word "lust" means "intense desire," which lures one into sin.

Satan knows our weaknesses and just when and how to attack Christians. It is our fault when we yield to him. We must take personal responsibility for our sins. It is our own selfish desire (the old nature) by which we are drawn away from God and enticed to sin. It is Satan's constant work to tempt God's children. The temptation is not sin, but the yielding is. Through Jesus Christ it is possible for us who have the tendency to sin to say "yes" to Jesus and "no" to Satan.

What can we do to overcome for ourselves and others?

1. We must acknowledge that there is a real devil.
2. We must learn to recognize him.
3. We must know his wiles and how to resist him.
4. We must call on Jesus for help, for "greater is he that is

in . . . [us] than he that is in the world" (I John 4:4). Jesus in us is closer than our hands and feet.

5. We must use the Scriptures as Jesus did on the mount of temptation.

Before a small evening Bible class, held in a home in Pennsylvania years ago, four of us had dinner together. One person, a stranger, had been invited to come because she was supposed to be "spiritual" and needed Christian fellowship. It was immediately evident to the three of us who were with her at the table that there was something odd about the young woman. She told us she belonged to a group in California called "The Truth." As she said that we each felt the power of Satan in the dining room.

All efforts at conversation were impossible. She knew nothing of the Christianity we were expressing. We spent the next thirty minutes trying to eat our dinner, quoting verse after verse of Scripture, giving her no opportunity to talk, because she had such a strange effect on us. Our only weapon was the Word of God and we used it.

Then two of us excused ourselves from the table to flee upstairs for special prayer, asking God for protection, for deliverance, and for the power of the blood of Christ from hindering me as I taught the lesson. (I had a very hard lesson that night and it turned out that we had our largest audience.)

While we were upstairs, the colored maid found excuses to stay in the dining room because she was afraid to leave the other guest alone with the very strange young cultist.

Satan got nowhere that night. God answered our prayers. At the end of the Bible study, the Devil tried to use the "possessed" young woman to "help" a very distressed lady who was there for the first time, by giving her all sorts of unscriptural tracts and literature. That accomplished nothing, for which we thanked God.

God's Word, the prayer of faith, the victory Christ won over Satan as we stood united in Him against the Devil, worked the deliverance that night.

6. We must "put on the whole armour of God" (Ephesians 6:11).

In Romans 13:12 we are told to "put on the armour of light" and in verse 14 to "put . . . on the Lord Jesus Christ." He is our armour for all parts of our bodies: loins, breasts, feet, arms, head, and all vulnerable parts (Ephesians 6:13-17).

Our enemy is powerful (verse 12). We need to take the whole armour (Christ) in order "to withstand in the evil day." There is no armour for the back. We are never to run from Satan but to stand in Christ against him "and having done all, to stand."

7. We must claim victory over Satan through the blood of Christ (Revelation 12:11). We must pray always in the Spirit for all saints (saved people) who are preaching the gospel to share with them in the battle against the evil one (Ephesians 6:18, 19).

Soldiers of Christ, arise,
And put your armor on,
Strong in the strength which God supplies
Through His eternal Son;
Strong in the Lord of Hosts,
And in His mighty power,
Who in the strength of Jesus trusts
Is more than conqueror.

Stand then in His great might,
With all His strength endued,
And take to arm you for the fight,
The panoply (protection) of God.
That having all things done,
And all your conflicts passed,
Ye may o'er-come through Christ alone,
And stand entire at last.

Leave no unguarded place,
No weakness of the soul;
Take every virtue, every grace,
And fortify the whole.
From strength to strength go on,
Wrestle and fight and pray;
Tread all the powers of darkness down,
And win the well-fought day.

While I have been working on this chapter, I have been very conscious of the opposition, of the powers of darkness working against me. A niece phoned me by long distance one night to ask me what was the matter; she had been compelled to pray for the Lord's strength and deliverance for me. I told her of my problem and thanked her for the help and relief which came from her faithfulness in prayer.

Satan never bothers unbelievers. They are in his kingdom; so he leaves them alone. If we are true Christians we are the objects of his "fiery darts."

Can you stand trials? James says: " . . . count it all joy when you fall into divers temptations [testings]" (James 1:2); "Blessed is the man that endureth temptation, for when he is tried, he shall receive the crown of life, which the Lord hath promised to them that love him" (James 1:12).

Peter says in I Peter 1:6, " . . . ye greatly rejoice . . .in heaviness through manifold temptations [testings]."

Very few of us can honestly say that we rejoice in testings, but, according to Peter in verse 7, "the trial of your faith, being much more precious than of gold that perisheth, though it be tried with fire, might be found unto praise and honour and glory at the appearing of Jesus Christ."

Someone has said about trials, "The hotter the water, the better and stronger is the tea."

We should welcome trials and testings and learn, as Paul did, always to "triumph in Christ . . . in every place" (II Corinthians 2:14).

The Christian's position is in Christ "in heavenly places" (Ephesians 2:6). He is not like a man in a valley struggling to reach the top of the hill, but like a man on the top of the hill fighting to maintain his position there against enemies who are trying to drag him down. The thing to do is to stay above Satan, in Christ, and through Christ's victory and power to refuse to yield one inch to the devil.

> My soul, be on thy guard;
> Ten thousand foes arise;
> The hosts of sin are pressing hard
> To draw thee from the skies.

"Let us therefore come boldly unto the throne of grace, that we may obtain mercy, and find grace to help in time of need" (Hebrews 4:16).

At the moment of assault, whenever the flaming temptation comes, turn to Christ with a cry for help, and the grace of God will be there in the nick of time.

Ah! whither could we flee for aid,
When tempted, desolate, dismayed;
Or how the hosts of hell defeat,
Had suffering saints no mercy seat?

There, there on eagle wings we soar,
And sin and sense molest no more;
And heaven comes down our souls to greet,
While glory crowns the mercy seat.

CHAPTER TEN

Toward

The Future—God's Eternal Home

The future—what is it for a Christian? The dictionary tells us the "future" is "what will happen; what is going to be; no one can foretell the future."

I do not want to contradict the writer of the dictionary, but we know the Bible tells us a great deal about future events and future places and what Christians can look forward to.

People in all generations have been interested in finding out what the future holds for them.

It is so today. Thousands of dollars and many hours are spent with fortune tellers, with mediums in witchcraft, with spiritualists in seances, or with ouija boards.

These practices are forbidden in the Scriptures. (Read Deuteronomy 18:9-14.) God here warns his people in verses 10 and 11 against those who do these things. He alone knows what is going to happen in their lives and wants His followers to walk by faith and trust Him.

To use "divination" is to try to tell the future by occult (mystic) means. Usually people want to know about love, marriage, and money. Politicians want to know how to vote. Gamblers want to know where to place their bets. A true Christian asks and trusts God to lead in all legitimate personal matters.

To be "an observer of times" is to believe in astrology, a pseudo science claiming to foretell the future by studying the supposed influence of the relative positions of the moon, sun, and stars on human affairs. To read a horoscope seriously is an attempt to learn by the month of your birth what will be your destiny. In our local newspaper is a daily column "Your Horoscope" by Jeanne Dixon.

It foretells what you should do; what you are like; how you should behave; and what you should expect because you were born under a certain constellation. This is forbidden by God, who holds our destiny in His hands. He has predestinated us to be His children (Ephesians 1:5) and to be conformed to the image of His Son (Romans 8:29).

An "enchanter" is one who uses omens, or lucky charms, to guide or to protect; or sorcery and witchcraft to cast an evil spell. God wants us to trust Him to guide and protect us. He gives us His Spirit to keep us free from an evil spirit.

A "charmer" is one who uses incantations to allure, or enchant a person to come under his or her power as does a snake charmer with a snake. God wants us to be under the power and control of the Holy Spirit.

"A consulter of familiar spirits" (a medium) or a "wizard," who practices black magic, must be left alone.

To delve into the spirit world is dangerous and harmful. King Saul found this out when he consulted the witch of Endor, asking her to bring up Samuel (I Samuel 28:7-11). In verse 15 Samuel asked Saul why he had brought him (his spirit) up. Saul replied that God had departed from him and would not answer him any more. Then Samuel told Saul that because of his disobedience the kingdom would be taken from him and given to David (verse 17). In I Chronicles 10:13 we are told that Saul died for disobeying God's word and for asking counsel of a medium.

From this account we learn of God's ways and should take warning. His presence is with obedient believers and His ear is open to their cry.

A "necromancer" is the last name listed in Deuteronomy 18:11, 12. This is a person who claims to be able to foretell the future by communing with the dead. Many people today who have lost loved ones in death try to receive help and comfort by going to one who practices necromancy. They want to feel a closeness to the one who has died or to find answers to questions and solutions to problems.

This is really selfish. The spirit of Samuel said to Saul, "Why hast thou disquieted me to bring me up?" (I Samuel 28:15). Samuel's work was done. He was at rest with the Lord.

The believing departed are at rest, happy, and peaceful in their Lord's presence. They should not be troubled or "disquieted" by the problems and unhappiness on earth. Those of us who are still down here are to turn to God for the answers and solutions, to Him, in whose presence our loved ones "in Christ" are happy.

All who did the things mentioned in Deuteronomy 18:10, 11 were abomination unto the Lord (verses 9, 12). The Israelites were not to learn to do these things (verse 9). The Lord "hath not suffered [or allowed] them so to do" (verse 14). Therefore, in Deuteronomy 20:13-18, God commanded the Israelites to completely destroy the heathen nations, lest His people become like them in their abominable practices.

In the New Testament, as the apostles preached to the Gentiles on their missionary journeys, they found the people committing these same sins.

We have the story in Acts 13:6-8 of a sorcerer, a false prophet, who withstood Saul and Barnabas at Paphos on the Island of Crete. This man, whose name was Bar-jesus, or Elymas, was a Jew. He did not want the deputy of the country to hear the word of God from Barnabas and Saul and be saved. Saul, filled with the Spirit, condemned the man's actions and, with the disciplining hand of the Lord upon him, the sorcerer was struck blind for a season (Acts 13:11). What was the result of this act? "Then the deputy, when he saw what was done, believed, being astonished at the doctrine of the Lord" (verse 12).

Here was a Jew, Bar-jesus, who knew God's laws from childhood, yet turned from his faith and worked to "pervert the . . . ways of the Lord" (verse 10).

In Acts 16:16-18 "a certain damsel [maid] possessed with a spirit of divination" met Paul and Silas as they went to prayer at Philippi. For many days she followed the men, crying, "These men are the servants of the most high God, which shew unto us the way of salvation." This grieved Paul, who recognized this as demon possession. He commanded the spirit to come out and "he came out the same hour." This girl was probably a Gentile, who had never known God's laws and was being used to raise money for her masters. She was delivered, and may have been saved, because she expressed her faith in the message of salvation as preached by God's servants. Perhaps she even became a member of the church at Philippi.

In Acts 19:18, 19, we have the account of many of the new believers at Ephesus being convicted of the sin of having in their possession curious books of black magic, which they had been practicing. They confessed this and showed their deeds. Then they brought their magical books and arts, which, after counting the price ($10,000 in our money), they burned publicly in a bonfire before all men. What was the result? "So mightily grew the word of God, and prevailed" (Acts 19:20).

In Ephesians 2:1-3, Paul reminded the Ephesians of their past when they "were dead in trespasses and sins"; when they walked according to "the spirit that now worketh in the children of disobedience [Satan] . . . in the lusts of [the] flesh [self], fulfilling the desires of the flesh and of the mind."

God, who loved them with a great love, had saved them from that old life to walk in a new life in Christ, doing good works (Ephesians 2:4, 5, 10).

We are warned about "seducing spirits, and doctrines [teaching] of devils" (I Timothy 4:1). What could be "seducing" (or deluding) spirits and doctrines of devils (demoniac teaching) other than false teaching of God's whole truth, including spiritism?

In II Timothy 3:13 we are warned that "evil men and seducers shall wax [become] worse and worse, deceiving, and being deceived." This passage is referring to the latter days of the church age, in which we are living.

The reason I have spent so much time on this subject in the early part of this chapter is that spiritism is very prevalent in our day. Even some who call themselves Christians are turning to the practice of these things. God has forbidden this for their own good. No nation has prospered or ever will prosper very long when this evil is active in the population.

Isaiah has the answer for us in chapter 8. In verse 11 he writes of the Lord speaking to him, telling him not to walk in the ways of the godless, but, in verse 17, to "wait upon the Lord [in prayer]" and "look for him." In verse 19 he tells the people (and us) not to listen to anyone who suggests that they try to find out the future by seeking mediums or "wizards that peep [whisper], and that mutter." The people (and we) should turn to a living God, to His Word the Bible, not to those who wrongly try to get a message from the dead.

The Spirit of God is "the Spirit of truth." Jesus said, " . . . he will guide you into all truth . . . and he will shew you things to come" (John 16:13).

160

The truth is that there is "heaven" ahead for every child of God. Jesus, who came down from heaven and went back to heaven, talked to Nicodemus, a highly educated, religious Jew about heaven. In John 3:13 Jesus mentioned the word "heaven" three times. It was where He had come from and where He would return to.

A young, liberal minister told his congregation one Sunday morning that he did not know whether there was a heaven or a hell. If there was a heaven he did not know whether it was a "place" or whether it was "up" or "down." "That did not matter." The people were shocked. They talked among themselves after church and, with help from some who knew their Bibles, found that heaven was "up" and it was a "place."

All through the Bible, heaven is called God's dwelling place. In Isaiah 66:1 the Lord said, "The heaven is my throne and the earth is my footstool." This verse is quoted by Stephen in Acts 7:49.

Moses told God's people in Deuteronomy 26:15 to ask God to "look down from thy [His] holy habitation, from heaven, and bless thy [His] people."

In II Chronicles 6:21, and again in verse 30, Solomon asks God: "Hear thou from thy dwelling place, even from heaven." In chapter 7, verse 14, the Lord replies with a familiar and important word that if His people humble themselves, pray, seek His face, and turn from their wicked ways, He will hear from heaven.

Jesus called heaven "God's throne" in Matthew 5:34. In Luke 3:22 "a voice came from heaven, which said, Thou art my beloved Son; in thee I am well pleased."

In Matthew 5:16 Jesus spoke of glorifying your Father which is in heaven, and in verse 48 said, "Be ye therefore perfect, even as your Father which is in heaven is perfect."

In the familiar Lord's Prayer, Jesus taught His disciples to pray to "Our Father which art in heaven." In John 17:1 Jesus "lifted up his eyes to heaven and said, Father." In Acts 1:9-11 Jesus was "taken up" into heaven (notice that the direction was "up"); the disciples looked toward heaven as He went "up," and the two men who stood by said, " . . . this same Jesus which is taken up from you into heaven . . . ."

In John, chapter 6, Jesus told the people who followed Him, asking many questions about Himself and His miracles, that He had come "down" from heaven to do His Father's will (verse 38).

161

In verses 39 and 40 Jesus told His listeners what the will of God was—that everyone who believed in Him would have everlasting life and would be raised up again "at the last day." Twice He used the words "at the last day." Jesus came "down" that believers might one day be taken "up" to be with Him.

One of our most familiar Scriptures on this subject (the future) is John 14:1-6. Here Jesus spoke of "my Father's house . . . [with] many mansions." "My Father's house" is heaven. In the many mansions (homes) there will be plenty of room.

Then Jesus said, "I go to prepare a place for you." This is a special place, a home, that Jesus, the bridegroom, is preparing for His bride, the church.

When the home is ready He "will come again." When He comes again (this is still in the future) He will receive (take) His own unto Himself, as a groom takes his bride to be his own, to live with him in his own home.

> In garments glorious He will come to open wide the door;
> And I shall enter my heavenly home, to dwell forevermore.[5]

We know that our heavenly home is an eternal one. It will be durable and secure. There will be no moths to destroy, no rust to corrupt and no thieves to break in or steal (Matthew 6:20). We know it will also be a place of no more tears, death, sorrow, crying, or pain (Revelation 21:4). There will be no more violence (verse 8), filthiness, evil, or dishonesty (Revelation 22:11). There will be no more curse (22:3) and no night (darkness) there (Revelation 22:5) and no more sea (21:1) to separate peoples.

Well, what will it be positively? What will be the quality of life we will have through all eternity and in what kind of surroundings will we live?

It will be a perfect home with those who love perfectly. It will be beautiful beyond our imagination. The environment will be exactly suited to our resurrected bodies (no polluted air or water). There will be perfect love, perfect joy, perfect peace, perfect knowledge, perfect wisdom, perfect righteousness, perfect purity, perfect fairness, perfect fellowship, perfect happiness, and perfect service.

There will be activity for all who go to heaven. We are told in Revelation 22:3 that "his servants shall serve him." A very athletic

Christian leader once said, "If heaven is a place where I'd have to sit on the edge of a pink cloud and play a harp forever, I wouldn't want to go there. But the Bible tells me I will serve the Lord forever, and that is what I shall enjoy." This will be perfect service in a perfect place. How wonderful! There will be no hindrance of any kind, but complete satisfaction in doing God's will. There will be complete fulfillment of our personalities and complete provision—everything human beings are looking for and failing to find here on earth.

It was just as I was preparing to write this chapter that my older brother Stewart died of heart disease. He had been sick a long time; so his death was not a surprise. The night before he died I talked to him over the telephone at his home in Pennsylvania. He sounded very ill, weak, and disappointed because he could not do any of the things that interested him. After the phone call, I felt so distressed I asked the Lord, that, if it was His will and my brother was ready to go, He would take him to heaven. If he was not ready, I asked that the Holy Spirit would please do the necessary work in his heart. The next morning the call came that he had died from a sudden attack around eight o'clock. I felt sad, but I thanked the Lord for the complete answer to my prayer, and was comforted.

Because of severe allergies I was not able to go to the funeral. The day after Stewart's death I was walking alone around our beautiful grounds at Camp Nathanael, in the Kentucky Mountains, when suddenly there came to me the consciousness of my brother's personality—completely free, satisfied, happy, and joyous in the light of the presence of His Savior. It seemed as if he was gladly saying, "I'm here, Ruth, I'm here!" The body of the brother I had always known was dead (worn out) and would be buried, but his human spirit and soul were intensely alive forevermore. His personality was completely fulfilled as never before, made possible only by the saving power of Jesus Christ. All that day, in my heart and mind I shared this joy, light, and life that my brother was experiencing and I was thrilled.

I did not ask for or expect this revelation from God. It would have been presumption to do so. The Lord gave it to me and I was grateful. For the first time in my life I realized what a great and sudden change comes to a believer when he goes to be with Christ. From Friday morning to Saturday morning, to me, Stewart had

163

changed from a weak, sick, disappointed person to the same man, the same personality, with the likeness or nature of Christ, and entirely happy in his eternal home. He had been dedicated to God by his parents before he was born, and God had answered their prayers. They were together in heaven with my sister, Baby May, who had died with diphtheria at the age of five, waiting for the day when "by and by the circle" would "be unbroken."

Heaven will be beautiful beyond our imagination. There will be no disappointment there—no failure to come up to our expectations.

In Revelation 21 John, the beloved disciple, gave us his description of "the holy city, new Jerusalem, coming down from God out of heaven, prepared as a bride adorned for her husband" (verse 2). This city has the glory of God in it (verse 11). The Lord God almighty and the Lamb are the temple of it. No temple or building will be needed for worship (Revelation 21:22). The Lord God and the Lamb will be present everywhere for us to worship and praise. When Christ came down to earth for a short time, He was "Immanuel, God with us." In the heavenly city it will be "us with God forever."

The Lamb is the light of that holy city. There is no need of sun, moon, or artificial lights to shine in it (Revelation 21:23).

John described the city as being very large, foursquare, and decorated with the most valuable and glittering ornaments of gold and precious stones. Although John did his best to give us a picture of what he saw, we know that this city was beyond description.

There are places on earth that are hard to describe. A man, Walt Disney, created with his imagination and ability two places that are attracting millions of visitors from all over the world. Those who come to the newly opened Walt Disney World, near Orlando, Florida, come away saying, "It's fantastic, perfectly beautiful, amazing, delightful, out-of-this-world and impossible to describe." If a mere man can produce such a happy place on earth, why should anyone question the ability of God to create something that really is beyond our imagination—a new heaven and a new earth (Isaiah 65:17) and a holy city prepared as a dwelling place for very special people, His very own.

There are to be twelve gates to this city. No entrance fees or tickets will be needed as at Disney World. The cost of all tickets

164

has been paid by the Lord Jesus Christ. We who have accepted His invitation to "come" can enter freely through those gates to be forever with Him. The gates will never close as those at Walt Disney World do at the end of every day, for visitors must leave and pay to get in again, if they want to return another day. No one will ever be forced out or locked out of the holy city. No wicked person will be allowed to enter this city, only those whose names are written in the Lamb's book of life (Revelation 21:27).

This heavenly city will be a happy place. The throne of God and of the Lamb will be in it (Revelation 22:3); and we "shall see His face" (verse 4; I Corinthians 13:12).

The story is told of a little boy whose family was very poor. He received no gifts at Christmas time, but he spent what time he could looking through the store windows at the pretty things other little boys could have. One day he was run over by a car and taken to a hospital. One of the nurses bought him a toy. As he touched it he said delightedly, "There isn't any glass between!"

Not only will we see the Lord face to face but we will know even as we are known. Now we are known by God (I Corinthians 8:3; Galatians 4:9). Then we will know Him as He really is.

When my life work is ended,
And I cross the swelling tide,
When the bright and glorious morning I shall see;
I shall know my Redeemer when I reach the other side,
And His smile will be the first to welcome me.

Oh, the soul-thrilling rapture when I view His blessed face,
And the luster of His kindly beaming eye;
How my full heart will praise Him for the mercy, love and grace,
That prepares for me a mansion in the sky.

Then let us trust God and Jesus Christ for a happiness to come, the lasting happiness of heaven. That happiness will make amends for the troubles we have endured down here. What God does is always good and right. We have His Word that there will be room for us all, and we will be entirely satisfied because Jesus, the Perfect Man, will be there. He has made heaven possible for us. Without His presence heaven would have no meaning. He "loved us, and washed us from our sins in his own blood" (Revelation 1:5).

165

The invitation is still open to all men, "Let him that is athirst come. And whosoever will, let him take the water of life freely" (Revelation 22:17). This is Jesus' invitation: "If any man thirst, let him come unto me and drink [take Him in]" (John 7:37); " . . . the water that I shall give him shall be in him a well of water springing up into everlasting life" (John 4:14).

The holy city as our eternal dwelling place is still far in the future. Before we can be established in it there are other events to take place. The next event on God's calendar for the Christian is the coming of Jesus for His own. He told His disciples, ". . . I will come again, and receive you unto myself that where I am there ye may be also" (John 14:3).

Many Christians since the day Christ ascended into heaven have looked forward to His return with hope and joy. They have not yet had their hope fulfilled. Death has overtaken them, but the promise has not changed.

The date of Christ's return is not known. Only God, the Father, knows when His Son will come to receive His own. The following are references concerning his coming:

> Acts 1:11—" . . . this same Jesus . . . shall so come in like manner as ye have seen him go into heaven."
> I Thessalonians 4:16, 17—"For the Lord himself shall descend . . . and the dead in Christ shall rise first: Then we which which are alive and remain shall be caught up together with them in the clouds, to meet the Lord in the air: and so shall we ever be with the Lord."
> II Thessalonians 2:1—" . . . the coming of our Lord Jesus Christ and . . . our gathering together unto him."

Here we are told that Jesus will come again as He went to heaven—in a cloud. He will catch up all believers, whether living or dead, in the clouds to meet Him in the air—to be forever with Him. This will be our "gathering together" to Him as a man gathers his harvest of grain, fruit, or whatever is ripe and ready for himself.

What will happen to us physically at His coming? Paul in I Corinthians 15:51, 52 tells us that "we shall all be changed." The bodies of believers who have died will be raised incorruptible, never to decay again. The mortals (those who are still living on earth) will put on immortality, never to die physically. The Lord Jesus will change our vile (lowly) bodies—bodies that are born to die a natural death—and fashion (make) them like "his glorious body" (Philippians 3:20, 21). John tells us, " . . . we know that, when he shall appear, we shall be like him; for we shall see him as he is" (I John 3:2).

From these verses in I Corinthians, Philippians, and I John we learn that our bodies will be changed to new, perfect bodies that we will have forever. They will be bodies that will be made like Jesus' own glorified, resurrected body—perfectly beautiful and healthy. We shall have a spiritual body, like Christ's, completely filled and empowered by the Holy Spirit (I Corinthians 15:42-44).

To sum this up: Every Christian will be changed, never to die again or, if living, never to die at all. Every Christian will have a new body, incorruptible and immortal, like Christ's resurrected body—transformed, spiritual, glorious. Every Christian will see Him as He is and will be like Him in His nature—pure and Spirit-filled.

The return of Christ for His own should not be looked upon as an escape from troubles, but as a comforting and exciting hope.

The best is yet to be for every Christian. What a glorious future and what a blessed hope! "Looking for that blessed hope, and the glorious appearing of the great God and our Saviour Jesus Christ" (Titus 2:13).

> It may be at morn, when the day is awaking,
> When sunlight through darkness and shadow is breaking,
> That Jesus will come in the fullness of glory,
> To receive from the world "His own."
>
> Oh, joy! oh, delight! should we go without dying,
> No sickness, no sadness, no dread and no crying,
> Caught up through the clouds with our Lord into glory,
> When Jesus receives "His own."

Those who have the new nature, the divine nature, Christ's own nature in them can look forward minute by minute to His coming. Those who have His nature will respond to His call and will go immediately to meet Him in the air.

My father used to illustrate this "blessed hope" by taking visitors (and sometimes I went along) to the huge scrap pile in the steel plant. He always carried gold, silver, nickel, and copper coins in his pocket.

At his signal a crane operator would move a large electric magnet toward the pile of a variety of metal scraps. Then Father would take the coins out of his pocket and throw them on top of the pieces of scrap. He would tell his guests to watch his coins to see what would happen to them. The magnet then would be lowered over the scrap pile, the electricity (power) would be turned on and, suddenly, pieces of iron would jump from the pile to the magnet which caught and held them. The gold coin, the silver coin, the nickel and copper coins remained unmoved. Only the pieces of scrap iron, which had the same nature as the magnet, responded to its drawing power. They were caught up, held, and carried away by the magnet to a special place prepared to receive them.

The return of Christ for His own is something wonderful to anticipate. After this event many of us believe there will be a very difficult time on earth for seven years, before He will return with His own to rule and reign on the earth for one thousand years.

During the interim between His coming for His own and later with His own to reign, there will be for every believer the events of the Judgment Seat of Christ (II Corinthians 5:10) and the Marriage Supper of the Lamb (Revelation 19:7-9). Every believer will appear before the Judgment Seat of Christ to be judged according to what he has done in his body while on earth—"whether it be good or bad." The Marriage Supper of the Lamb will take place when the bride has made herself ready. Christ will celebrate this wonderful union of all believers with Himself before He will return to rule and reign as King over the earth. The Scriptures seem to indicate that faithful believers will help Him in His reign. I like to think He will want to share the responsibilities of His reign with those who have proved themselves to be faithful and obedient while on earth.

This thousand-year reign on earth will be a great event in the world. The best is yet to be not only for every true Christian, but also for this troubled, restless, war-torn world when a righteous King will be on the throne of David in Jerusalem. What a marvelous thought this is!

168

The Old Testament foretold the coming of a Savior and King. He was to be a Jew, of the tribe of Judah, a descendant of David the king, born in Bethlehem, born of a virgin. He was to rule and reign over the nations of the world.

Jesus, the descendant of Abraham, the first Jew, the descendant of David of the tribe of Judah, was born in Bethlehem of a virgin named Mary. He was of the royal line and was the only man who had the right to reign. He was called "King of the Jews" by Wise Men. He was announced by angels to shepherds as their Savior, Christ, the Lord. "But when the fulness of the time was come, God sent forth his Son, made of a woman . . . " (Galatians 4:4). To that woman, Mary, the angel Gabriel appeared (Luke 1:26-33), telling her some amazing things. God had chosen her, a virgin, to be the mother of His Son as Isaiah, the prophet, had foretold in chapter 7, verse 14. Mary was to call His name "Jesus." He would be "great" and would be called "the Son of the Highest." The Lord God would give Him "the throne of his father David," and He would "reign over the house of Jacob for ever." There would never be an end to His kingdom.

Jesus was called great and the Son of the Highest during His short three and one-half years of public ministry, but His own Jewish people rejected Him as their king. The last part of Gabriel's promise to Mary has not yet been fulfilled. Jesus has yet to sit on David's throne, ruling over the house of Jacob, all the twelve tribes of Israel.

According to I Timothy 6:15 "in his times he shall shew, who is the blessed and only Potentate, the King of kings, and Lord of lords."

Jeremiah prophesies of the day when Jerusalem will be called "the throne of the Lord; and all the nations shall be gathered unto it, to the name of the Lord, to Jerusalem: neither shall they walk any more after the imagination of their evil heart" (Jeremiah 3:17).

In Micah 4:1-5 we are told of a glorious time when Jerusalem will be the capital of the world and the Lord will rule the nations from there.

Isaiah writes in chapter 24:23 of the glorious reign of the Lord of Hosts in Jerusalem before His ancient people (the Jews); and in Isaiah 33:20, 21 he tells us Jerusalem will be "a quiet habitation" and "the glorious Lord will be unto us a place of broad rivers and streams." (This will be quite a contrast to a city torn by strife and a place which has never had an abundance of water.) The Lord will be the judge, lawgiver, and king. His rule will be righteous, fair, and powerful.

> Jerusalem, the golden, With milk and honey blest!
> Beneath thy contemplation, Sink heart and voice oppressed.
> I know not, O I know not, What joys await us there;
> What radiancy of glory, What bliss beyond compare.

> There is the throne of David; And there, from care released,
> The song of them that triumph, The shout of them that feast;
> And they who with their Leader Have conquered in the fight,
> Forever and forever Are clad in robes of white.

This will be the time when for a thousand years there will be peace on earth. Men "shall beat their swords into plowshares, and their spears into pruninghooks." They shall not "learn war any more" (Isaiah 2:4).

In the book of Revelation we read in chapter 20 of this thousand-year reign of Christ on earth, when those who take part in the first resurrection (at His first coming) will reign with Him (Revelation 20:6). Satan will be bound and there will be an orderly, disciplined rule by One who will know how to rule mankind "with a rod of iron" (Revelation 2:27) and yet with love. What a glorious prospect that is for the earth!

For those who have died before Christ comes to take His own to heaven, the future is bright. The New Testament teaches us that "to die is gain" (Philippians 1:21); to be absent from the body is to be "present [in soul and spirit] with the Lord" (II Corinthians 5:8). "To depart, and to be with Christ" is "far better" than staying here on earth (Philippians 1:23).

Just recently I was told of the home-call of a friend, one of God's faithful servants. He was in a hospital slowly dying of terminal cancer. In the same room was one other patient. This man heard my friend suddenly say, "God?" Then came his question, "Yes?" Then again, "God!" and with a radiant smile he was unexpectedly gone, called home by his Lord.

Some people love this world too much to want to leave it. In contrast to the other story, a few days later a woman in a beauty

170

shop told those present that her husband would not play golf any more. Although he loved the game and had nothing wrong with his heart, he was afraid to get out on the golf course for fear he would have an attack and die. He wanted to stay down here on earth as long as possible. This was his home.

Even Christians can be afraid of death, but they should not be. Christ has taken away the sting of death, which is sin (I Corinthians 15:56). When we think of the word "sting" our minds see some sort of insect, usually a bee. The sting of a mosquito can cause serious illness (malaria, sleeping sickness) and the sting of a bee can cause sudden death.

Some years ago I was asked to give some Bible messages during the morning service at the then pastorless Presbyterian Church at Wooton, Kentucky. It was in the early fall, the windows were open, and very active wasps were flying in and out of the building. Suddenly, as I was in the middle of my talk, I felt something strange around a triple strand of beads on my neck. Automatically I placed my hand there to feel the beads. As I touched them I felt a sharp sting and saw a wasp fly away to an open window. The immediate reaction was a hot, tingly sensation as if every nerve end in my body was on fire. I kept on talking, for the people seemed to be listening, and I managed to act as if nothing had happened.

However, I found myself doing double talk. Audibly I kept talking to the congregation, and silently, in my heart, to my heavenly Father. I told Him I was not one bit afraid to die, for it would be wonderful to be with Him in heaven, but I thought the congregation would be very upset if I died right there. In my opinion it would really be a most inconvenient time and place to die. If it would please Him I would prefer to live a little longer.

For forty-eight hours I tingled day and night until the effect of the wasp's sting wore off. The next Sunday I was due to speak again at the same church. I dreaded being stung again. It was a temptation to ask to be excused, but I knew I must conquer the fear of those wasps. I asked the Lord for deliverance and victory. The answer was perfect: there was no fear; there were no wasps! And I had complete victory and perfect freedom in giving out God's Word.

Christ not only took away the sting of death, but He took upon Him the wrath of God against all sinners as He hung on the cross.

There are judgments to come. Many people, even Christians, are afraid of the judgment. John wrote in I John 4:15-18 that in the day of judgment (for judgment for all sinners is ahead: Revelation 20:11-15) those who love God and belong to Him will have boldness and not fear because of Christ's perfect love in dying for them. "There is no fear in love; but perfect love casteth out fear." Paul, in Colossians 2:13, 14 tells Christians that through Christ's death all trespasses have been forgiven, all the records of our sins that were against us have been blotted out, or erased, as a teacher uses an eraser to completely remove every chalk mark.

We can illustrate this by the two thieves dying on crosses near Jesus. One called Him "Lord" and was saved. The other derided Him and was lost. The unsaved thief will be afraid at the judgment. The saved thief will know no fear. His sins are gone forever.

> There is a fountain filled with blood
> Drawn from Immanuel's veins . . . .
> The dying thief rejoiced to see
> That fountain in his day.

Though the Scriptures promise dreadful times to come, when the judgment of God will fall on this world, the Christian can believe that the Lord will deliver him.

In the Old Testament Noah was delivered from the judgment of the flood because he was righteous; Lot was delivered from Sodom. Though a weak believer, Lot was called "just" and "righteous" (II Peter 2:7, 8). Rahab, the harlot, was delivered from the destruction of Jericho because of her faith in God (Hebrews 11:31).

We believe deliverance will come for us who are saved, when Christ comes back for His own and takes us away from the frightening times to come.

We have the warning that perilous times shall come (II Timothy 3:1-7, 13). When we hear, see, or read of the news of the world today, the words in these eight verses from II Timothy, chapter 3, sound very up-to-date.

The return of our Lord from heaven for His own can be our daily and blessed hope. Perhaps He will come today.

Jesus is coming to earth again, What if it were today? . . .
Coming to claim His chosen Bride, All the redeemed
and purified . . . .
Satan's dominion will soon be o'er . . . Sorrow and sighing shall
be no more. . . .
Then shall the dead in Christ arise, Caught up to meet Him
in the skies. . . .
Faithful and true would He find us here . . . Watching in
gladness and not in fear . . . .
Signs of His coming multiply . . . . Watch, for that time is
drawing nigh.
What if it were today?[6]

Very often the question is asked, "Will I know my loved ones in heaven?" Although Peter, James, and John had never seen Moses and Elias, they immediately recognized them as they talked to Christ on the Mount of Transfiguration. Paul made it plain in his message to the Thessalonians in I Thessalonians 4:13-18 that their loved ones who had died in Christ and whose souls and spirits were with Jesus in heaven God would bring with Christ when He returned for His own at His second coming (verse 14). "Then we which are alive and remain shall be caught up together with them in the clouds, to meet the Lord in the air; and so shall we ever be with the Lord" (verse 17). The word "together" is the answer to the question "Will we know our loved ones?" Yes, we will! "Wherefore comfort one another with these words" (verse 18).

> Not one person of God's Family;
> Not one member of Christ's Body;
> Not one stone in God's Building,
> Will be left behind when
> Christ comes for His own.

Now we come to the place of summing up our responsibility toward the Lord Jesus Christ to "act like Christians" as we wait daily for the shout and trumpet call.

In the light of His coming, "what manner of persons ought" we "to be in all holy conversation [daily living] and godliness" (II Peter 3:11)? Peter tells us in verse 14 to "be diligent that" we "may be found of him in peace, without spot, and blameless."

173

Here are some of the things we must do:

Love God with all our hearts. Mark 12:30
Love our neighbors as ourselves. Mark 12:31
Read, study, and obey Christ's commands. Luke 6:46
Love other Christians as Jesus loves us. John 15:12
Humbly serve one another as Christians. John 13:14, 15
Present our bodies to Him. Romans 12:1
Occupy till He comes; keep serving Him. Luke 19:13, 17
Be faithful. God requires this. I Corinthians 4:2
Be steadfast, unmoveable. I Corinthians 15:58
Rejoice, pray, give thanks. I Thessalonians 5:16-18
Be patient. James 5:8
Be humble. I Peter 5:6
Be strong in the Lord. Ephesians 6:10
Flee evil; follow good things. I Timothy 6:11
Fight the good fight of faith. I Timothy 6:12
Always triumph in Christ; make Him known in every place. II Corinthians 2:14
Purify our lives. I John 3:3
Walk (live daily) in love. Ephesians 5:2
Walk circumspectly (carefully). Ephesians 5:15
Walk in the Spirit. Galatians 5:16
Be filled with the Spirit. Ephesians 5:18
Seek heavenly things; set our affection above. Colossians 3:1, 2
Preach the Word diligently, constantly. II Timothy 4:2
Look for the blessed hope. Live soberly, righteously, and godly. Titus 2:12, 13
Read chapters 12 and 13 of Romans over and over again for the teaching of practical Christian behavior.
Abide in Christ (keep close to Him) in order not to be ashamed at His coming. I John 2:28, 29
Trust Him for our future. Do not worry about it. Matthew 6:34
Do not try to find out what will happen in our lives. When Jesus told Peter in John 21:18, 19 the kind of tragic death Peter would die, Peter wanted to know what was going to happen to John (verse 21). Jesus said to Peter, "What is that to thee? Follow thou me." In other words, He was saying: "You are responsible not for John's future but for your own life to live it My way."

To see Jesus, to be with Him, to be like Him, and to hear Him say, "Well done," will be worth it all.

God in His fairness and love promises rewards. We are told that "we must all appear before the judgment seat of Christ; that every one may receive the things done in his body, according to that he hath done, whether it be good or bad" (II Corinthians 5:10).

According to I Corinthians 3:14 a reward will be given to everyone whose work measures up to God's standards. On the foundation of faith in Jesus Christ (verse 11), men are building gold, silver, precious stones, wood, hay, stubble. Fire shall try each man's work to see of what sort it is (verse 13). If it burns up, the man will be saved but will receive no reward (verse 15). If his work stands the test he shall be rewarded. Each person will be satisfied with God's judgments. They will be fair.

What works will be burned up? What works will be rewarded? Anything done in the flesh (self), out of the will of God, without the power of the Holy Spirit, will not stand the fire. Everything done for Christ, in the will of God, through the power of the Holy Spirit will be rewarded.

In John, chapter 15, Jesus called His followers to bear "fruit," "more fruit," "much fruit"; "fruit" that "should remain." The secret of successful fruit bearing is the abiding life: they in Him and He in them. To me this means first my staying close to Him, in union with Him, with His Spirit filling my life to make me like Him. Then second it means my witnessing of Him to others to bring them to know Him as Savior and Lord. When people sense the presence of Christ in our lives and our knowledge of and obedience to His Word, they will listen to what we have to say.

It is Christmas Eve as I write these words. Tomorrow we celebrate the coming of the Lord Jesus Christ as a babe to Bethlehem. We look forward to the next event: His coming back for us to take us to be forever with Him.

Soon after that He will return with His own to rule and reign over the earth for one thousand years. A short period in history will follow and then will come the new heaven and the new earth and our glorious eternal home in the holy city, the new Jerusalem.

What will we do in heaven? We shall worship God and the Lamb (Revelation 4:10, 11; Revelation 5:9; 11-14). We shall have fellowship with God and His Son (Revelation 21:3, 22). He will be with us and we shall see His face (Revelation 22:4). We will serve

Him (Revelation 22:3). We shall be students, ever learning to know Him better, experiencing a growing knowledge of what Christ did for us (Ephesians 2:7), and receiving new revelations and explanations of God's dealings with us through circumstances and testings. We will have a growing understanding of His truths as hidden and revealed in the Bible. We will have all eternity to learn to know all the redeemed of all the ages and to enjoy the presence of all the unfallen angels of God.

Jesus was God's love gift to us. We will be His love gift to God when He will present us "faultless before the presence of his glory with exceeding joy" (Jude 24).

Therefore we should faithfully build up ourselves in our most holy faith, pray in the Holy Spirit, keep ourselves in the love of God, looking for eternal life, and pull others out of the fire (Jude 20-23).

We can then say with Jude, "To the only wise God our Saviour, be glory and majesty, dominion and power, both now and ever" (verse 25); and with John, in anticipation of the joys to come, "Even so, come, Lord Jesus" (Revelation 22:20).

Jesus may come today, Glad day! Glad day!

* * * * *

And I will freely tell Why I should love Him so well,
For He is my all today.

* * * * *

Glad day, Glad day! . . . I'll live for today, nor anxious be,
Jesus, my Lord, I soon shall see;
Glad day! Glad day! Is it the crowning day?

176

REFERENCES

1. "Thy Word Is a Lamp To My Feet," Ernest O. Sellers
   © Copyright 1908 by Ernest O. Sellers
   Renewal 1936 by Broadman Press
   All Rights Reserved
   Used by Permission

2. "I Would Be Like Jesus," James Rowe
   Copyright 1912 by E. O. Excell
   © Renewed 1940 (extended) by B. D. Ackley
   Assigned to The Rodeheaver Company
   Used by Permission

3. "All Things In Jesus," H. D. Loes
   Copyright by Hope Publishing Company
   Used by Permission

4. "Only Believe," Paul Rader
   Copyright 1921 by Paul Rader
   The Rodeheaver Company, Owner
   © Renewed 1949 by Mary C. Rader
   Assigned to The Rodeheaver Company
   Used by Permission

5. "Ivory Palaces," H. Barraclough
   Copyright by Hope Publishing Company
   Used by Permission

6. "What If It Were Today?" Leila N. Morris
   Copyright by Hope Publishing Company
   Used by Permission